NEGOTIATION AND CONFLICT RESOLUTION IN CRIMINAL PRACTICE

NEGOTIATION AND CONFLICT RESOLUTION IN CRIMINAL PRACTICE

A Handbook

Rebecca Jaremko Bromwich and Thomas Harrison

CANADIAN SCHOLARS

Toronto | Vancouver

Negotiation and Conflict Resolution in Criminal Practice: A Handbook
By Rebecca Jaremko Bromwich and Thomas Harrison

First published in 2019 by
Canadian Scholars, an imprint of CSP Books Inc.
425 Adelaide Street West, Suite 200
Toronto, Ontario
M5V 3C1

www.canadianscholars.ca

Library and Archives Canada Cataloguing in Publication

Title: Negotiation and conflict resolution in criminal practice : a handbook / Rebecca Jaremko Bromwich and Thomas Harrison.
Names: Bromwich, Rebecca, author. | Harrison, Thomas, 1966- author.
Identifiers: Canadiana (print) 20190172711 | Canadiana (ebook) 20190175524 | ISBN 9781773381480
    (softcover) | ISBN 9781773381497 (PDF) | ISBN 9781773381503 (EPUB)
Subjects: LCSH: Dispute resolution (Law)—Canada. | LCSH: Criminal law—Canada. | LCSH: Communication
    in law—Canada.
Classification: LCC KE8615 .B76 2019 | LCC KF9084 .B76 2019 kfmod | DDC 347.71/09—dc23

Page layout by S4Carlisle
Cover design by Rafael Chimicatti

Printed and bound in Ontario, Canada

Canada

This book is dedicated to Bartleby and all his heirs, devisees, representatives, successors, and assigns, as a hopeful gesture.

We would also like to acknowledge Professor Mark Weisberg, through whose ethics class at Queen's law school we became acquainted with Bartleby, and from whose wisdom and mentorship we have drawn a great deal of resilience for decades.

Special thanks are also due to Theo Gavrielides, who made a crucial contribution to Chapter 5 of this book by enriching it with his expertise in the area of restorative justice.

The authors also wish to acknowledge the support of our families in all of our endeavours.

The wise warrior avoids the battle.
—Sun Tzu, *The Art of War**

---

* *The Art of War* is an ancient Chinese text about military strategy, dating from the 5th century BCE, or what is known as the "Spring and Autumn Period."

CONTENTS

INTRODUCTION

The Context: Conflict Resolution and Negotiation in Criminal Law

Discourage litigation. Persuade your neighbors to compromise whenever you can. As a peacemaker the lawyer has superior opportunity of being a good man. There will still be business enough.
— Abraham Lincoln, "Notes for a Law Lecture," 1850

We've been involved in criminal justice for many years, practising as lawyers since 2002. During this period, we've observed that there remains, at best, a mismatch and, at worst, a troubling gap between the criminal law theory that we learned in school and its practice in the legal system. The typical justice system model uses formal procedures, epitomized in the courtroom trial, which emphasizes highly prescribed, oppositional roles for Crown and defence lawyers. These advocates act as adversaries to represent opposing parties to resolve criminal allegations. This description is a common depiction of criminal law practice and procedure in Canada today.

Yet, in our experience, the vast majority of the work of criminal law occurs outside of trials, outside of court, and increasingly, using alternative processes. Most criminal lawyers rely on these alternatives to the more traditional adversarial paradigm. While the inherent dichotomy between criminal defence and prosecution remains, alternative procedures often require collaboration and do not always necessarily even emphasize the roles of counsel. In fact, there are a whole range of individuals in criminal justice whose participation in the resolution of disputes has become increasingly important in the effective operation of the justice system. Important additional participants include not only others who perform recognized advocacy roles, like paralegals, mediators, and social workers, but also the victims of crime, family members, and community representatives.

Our combined experiences, both before and after our calls to the Bar, have involved varied roles in Canadian criminal justice. This includes acting as counsel and paralegal advocates for the defence, social services, and teaching in various capacities, including now in academia. We have both served as Crown Counsel and have worked directly in court or to develop policy in relation to criminal proceedings. At law school, we primarily learned persuasive oral and written techniques designed for adversarial settings, in keeping with standard conceptions of lawyer roles. However, in our careers, we've found that criminal law practice involves a wide range of conflict resolution skills. This book is intended to address the gap we have perceived.

Our approach incorporates several different themes. It is the foundational premise of this book that, in the contemporary practical reality of criminal practice, there is a wide toolkit of conflict resolution skills, which are at least as important as persuasive advocacy typified by more formal, traditional argument. Consequently, one major goal of our work is to describe the important role of negotiation and other alterative conflict resolution techniques in Canadian criminal law. A further important theme is practicality. So, at the end of each chapter, we identify tips, techniques, strategies, and best practices to enhance the abilities of anyone working to resolve disputes through bargaining and other alternatives in Canadian criminal law.

We set the stage in the first part of this work by situating "negotiation" within the traditional criminal justice setting. There is a long tradition of "open courts" in Canada that has historically made all criminal proceedings publicly transparent.[1] This transparency ensures scrutiny in the public demonstration of fairness, justice, and protection of an accused person's rights before a third-party adjudicator, who hears matters in adherence with accepted standards of procedural regularity, before determining an outcome.

We also consider how all court proceedings are built on a presumption of adversarialism. Representatives of the parties control preparation and oppositional presentation of evidence to advance written and oral arguments in support of their clients. This inherent adversarialism in court proceedings is probably most apparent in criminal law,[2] since the emphasis in criminal justice is on protecting the public interest, as a forum designed to allow people to advance and defend their most basic rights, like liberty, security, and privacy.

The ubiquity of bargaining, for pleas but also for other purposes, at many different stages of criminal proceedings requires collaboration and a skill set of integrative competencies. Alternatives to traditional adversarialism in criminal matters also means that resolutions are increasingly occurring outside of court, and even outside of legal proceedings. Whether in court or through some alternative resolution process, other parties also play an increasingly acknowledged and often vital role to resolve criminal files.

Chapter 1 starts by addressing the practice and theory of negotiation in the context of Canadian criminal law. We set out approaches to negotiation in criminal justice, and illustrate some considerations in criminal law bargaining in a hypothetical negotiation. Our viewpoint favours collaborative bargaining, which we argue involves skills that can be acquired and enhanced. Within some limits, which we acknowledge and discuss, we believe a collaborative perspective, combined with some mindful attention to the development of an individual's particular negotiation style, has the most potential to best represent the interests of clients in criminal law proceedings.

Chapter 2 starts by considering the theory and practice of conflict resolution more generally, and then in criminal justice specifically. We scope out the major ethical and legal professionalism requirements imposed on lawyers in Canada in criminal law bargaining. Lawyers are expected to consider settlement, inform clients of options outside of formal justice processes when appropriate, and, if so instructed, take steps to pursue those options. Taken together, these obligations require advocates to strongly consider settling disputes, and in the criminal context, this means they are under ethical duties to consider plea bargaining. This text explores how ethical quandaries can present obstacles when criminal lawyers, acting either for the prosecution or for the defence, engage in these kinds of conflict resolution practices.

For example, this includes a consideration of privacy and confidentiality obligations to clients, which we also demonstrate in a hypothetical situation involving a resolution discussion between defence and prosecution. We also highlight the need for effective communication skills to represent clients, including the professional obligation of "civility" in Canadian law, which we further explore in a legal case study involving a British Columbia lawyer sanctioned for inappropriate professional conduct. We end the section by connecting the discussion about collaborative approaches and style in the first chapter to provide some practical suggestions to develop strategic skills in criminal law negotiations.

In part because of the prescribed roles of Crown and defence counsel, our initial emphasis in the first two chapters is on the functions of lawyers in these contexts. In considering challenges of negotiating across differences in **Chapter 3**, we identify and further discuss the systemic roles of advocates, especially in light of the adversarial imperative of criminal law. We identify several errors of cognition that can adversely affect those in these roles, which are further illustrated in a case study of the Donald Marshall wrongful conviction. The *Marshall* case also serves as a departure point for examining the importance of social context, and the need for cultural competency in negotiations. Procedural context and the capacity for technical abilities, especially in light of the expanded use of online communications and negotiation platforms in recent years, rounds out our look at bargaining across differences in criminal law. In this respect, we examine some of the potential benefits, but also the risks and pitfalls, of modern communications and provide some tips on the burgeoning use of new technologies in criminal law resolutions.

Though we look primarily at the roles of professional advocates through the first sections of the book, we also examine and underscore the importance of other participants in resolving criminal disputes, particularly in **Part II**, which starts by looking at alternative dispute resolution (ADR) and diversions in criminal law. **Chapter 4** examines the rise of ADR generally in Canadian law, its increasing use in criminal proceedings, and some specific professional and ethical considerations implicated in these alternative approaches. These considerations are illustrated by highlighting the use of alternatives and diversions where client capacity may be an issue and in instances involving youth.

For example, where "extrajudicial measures" and "extrajudicial sanctions" are provided for under Canada's youth crime laws, the ways in which offending behaviour is addressed through diversion outside of the formal system can have a profound and lasting impact on that youth's future employability, career, and life chances. We also examine victim-offender mediation, and present a recent case study that illustrates the potential for this alternative. In addition, we look at and critically assess the use of ADR in family law matters that also involve potential allegations of criminality, and end by providing some practical guidance in the implementation of alternative and diversionary procedures in all settings.

In **Chapter 5**, we expand our look at alternatives in criminal law to explore the theory and approaches of "restorative justice." This includes revisiting victim-offender mediation to identify its place within the broader restorative context, which has distinct connections to Canada's Indigenous communities. Restorative approaches employ multiple different practices, such as Family Group Conferencing, Healing/ Sentencing and Peacekeeping circles, and Community Restorative Boards (CRBs). Contemporary approaches to restorative justice got their start in Ontario, Canada, in a 1970s matter involving youth justice, which we also examine in closer detail in a more modern context. We then practically illustrate restorative justice approaches through a case study and discussion of a recent incident involving Nova Scotia's Restorative Justice Program. We set out some restorative justice standards and conclude with a brief critical comment on this expanding and innovative approach in Canadian law.

A final theme throughout the book, which we also emphasize in **Chapter 6**, underscores the importance of professional well-being, self-care, and work/life balance for all professionals working in criminal law. In this section, we turn more holistically to consider the lives of legal services professionals, suggesting ways forward to resolve workplace, interpersonal, work/life, and systemic conflicts that impact on both personal health and careers. We examine the widespread challenge of mental health in Canadian law, which has adversely affected the legal profession, but also many others who play important roles in implementing our system of criminal justice.

One important part of playing an effective role in criminal resolutions is the exercise of good judgement, which can become problematic when people are losing perspective and reasoning skills because of ill health. In our view, exercising self-care, seeking to enhance personal well-being, and working to support colleagues by encouraging healthy environments is a key competency to being a successful professional in the criminal law field. We also provide some suggestions to help deal with challenging client situations or aggressive and difficult people in the context of criminal law resolutions. The penultimate section expands our discussion to examine systemic challenges some face, which can influence individual behaviour and how it is perceived. Systemic issues include gender, religious beliefs, and racial discrimination. The last part presents a literary case study, summarizing Melville's novella *Bartleby the Scrivener* and discussing it light of modern concerns about professional well-being in law.

One of the most important premises in our work is that the practical reality of the criminal justice system is somewhat different from both what is commonly perceived and from what we learned in our legal educations. In many ways, our efforts in this book reflect a lot of the things we have learned through practice, and that we wish we had known better when we first started. In any role, facilitating or contributing to the effective resolution of criminal disputes requires some degree of professional and personal balance. Negotiation, collaborative professionalism, adaptability in using alternatives, communicating effectively, and other conflict resolution competencies are at least as important as more traditional persuasive and adversarial oral and written advocacy skills. A reflective sense of personal strengths, the capacity to understand our individual behaviour in situational and systemic context, and to mindfully assess our situation personally and as professionals is one key to overall success.

ENDNOTES

1. The "open courts" principle has considerable jurisprudential support in Canada, e.g., see *AG (Nova Scotia) v MacIntyre*; *Canadian Broadcasting Corp v New Brunswick (Attorney General)*, [1996] 3 SCR 480, at para 23.

2. In the standard conception of the lawyers' role, adversarialism in court proceedings is probably best justified in criminal law, because it involves disputes about these basic rights, as described by David Luban, "The Adversary System Excuse," in *Legal Ethics and Human Dignity*. Cambridge: Cambridge University Press, 2007, particularly at 32–64.

PART I

Conflict Resolution and Negotiation in Traditional Criminal Law Processes

CHAPTER 1

Negotiation: Principles, Theory, and Approach

LEARNING OBJECTIVES

After reading this chapter, students should have new insight into:

- The wide range of negotiations in criminal law
- Principled negotiation in theoretical context
- Developing an overall approach and some tactics for effective negotiation
- Applying the "Seven Steps to Principled Negotiation"
- Building on individual strengths to develop and leverage negotiating styles

OVERVIEW

This chapter situates negotiation in the context of justice system professionals, who bargain in criminal proceedings in Canada. It discusses overall approaches to negotiation theory and highlights research showing the benefits of planning in negotiation through the deliberate application of bargaining theory. Planning involves considering your approach to the process, incorporating an awareness of your own style in negotiation, and developing an organized strategy to improve outcomes and better protect client interests.

Our approach to bargaining identifies and explains a well-established framework from negotiation literature, which provides a "roadmap" to approach the distinct challenge of preparation in this area. This focus acknowledges the recent array of writing on negotiation theory and practice. However, the pragmatic purpose of this handbook means we focus on basic theory and prescription in the criminal law context, emphasizing "interest-based" negotiations as a good model to address criminal law matters.

Structuring negotiations can orient them in a way that increases the likelihood that the process will be more efficient and more effective. Our prescription for bargaining in criminal law draws on established concepts of principled negotiation to provide guidance, which can assist at various stages and in a wide range of negotiations. This chapter also sets out a hypothetical case study where readers can apply the elements of interest-based bargaining in practical circumstances and concludes by distinguishing negotiation "style" from theoretical approaches and strategy. A negotiator's personal style is an important factor that can leverage individual strengths and increase both the likelihood and quality of resolutions.

Our perspective is consistent with a view that sees negotiation as best conceived as a kind of conversation or discussion (Condlin), though structured in an organized way since it is intended to lead to some sort of agreement. Our emphasis on the functional role of non-adversarial, principled negotiations (Fisher and Ury) is in contrast to their primary alternative in negotiating theory, which are distributive approaches to negotiation. These alternative frameworks are characterized by their emphasis on competition, aggression, and inherent adversarialism (MacFarlane, 155–167).

Competitive negotiation behaviours have effects that are often counterproductive to clients, unduly reducing the complexity of interests at stake, and increasing litigation costs in way that also decreases the range of options available (Menkel-Meadow, 776). Though applying traditional and non-adversarial approaches to negotiation in the criminal context has some distinct features, we believe this approach has positive potential to effectively enhance mutually beneficial outcomes in criminal law (Hollander-Blumhoff, 1997). At appropriate points, alternative competitive approaches to negotiation along with further perspectives, some of which complement our characterization of principled bargaining, are also addressed.

NEGOTIATION IN THE CRIMINAL CONTEXT

The application of negotiation theory to criminal law has received scant study in the past. From a practical perspective, most legal professionals involved in bargaining in criminal proceedings receive little education or ongoing training in this area (Roberts and Wright). Legal education and continuing professional development usually focus instead on advocacy skills in formal proceedings, particularly in the context of legal trials. In our anecdotal experience, negotiation ability is often regarded as an inherent talent, something some lawyers are just "naturally good at." Success in criminal negotiations is also often not attributed to individual bargaining competency, but instead is seen as relying on the positive interpersonal relations between the prosecution and defence counsel.

In fact, negotiation has become a dominant feature of modern criminal proceedings. In our observation across a wide range of criminal contexts, a capacity to effectively bargain is a professional duty (FLSC, *Model Code*, 3.1-1 (c) (v)), whose competencies are employed, often daily, in the legal system. Support for the proposition beyond our personal experience can also be found in the comments of the Supreme Court of Canada, which recently confirmed that "resolution discussions between Crown and defence counsel are not only commonplace in the criminal justice system, they are essential. Properly conducted, they permit the system to function smoothly and efficiently" (*R v Anthony-Cook*, para 1).

The minimal literature addressing negotiation in criminal law supports the view that this process is ubiquitous. Research also runs contrary to a view that bargaining predominantly depends on the importance of interpersonal contacts between prosecution and defence counsel. While we make the case that establishing and maintaining good relations is an important professional consideration that fits within the theoretical model of principled bargaining, it is important to note that some research has shown that effective bargaining outcomes do not necessarily rely on good relations between lawyers (Doyel). As with most skills, while there are likely some who have natural interpersonal skills and bargaining ability, the deliberate development and use of negotiation strategies and techniques, like those outlined in this book, can demonstrably improve results (Schneider). This handbook builds on these observations to regard effective bargaining in criminal law as a skill that can be both learned and enhanced.

A better understanding of the dynamics of negotiation along with practical tools developed can help lawyers, paralegals, and other professionals working in the criminal justice system navigate the many kinds of negotiations they will face. While there are a wide range of circumstances in which negotiations occur, much of this chapter focuses on those between counsel in resolution discussions through agreed pleadings, commonly known as a "plea bargain." Much of plea bargaining involves a situation where third-party arbiters are either not involved or are only peripheral to the negotiation process. Negotiations that involve a third, neutral party, and related procedures like mediation, arbitration, and restorative justice circles are examined more closely in Chapter 4 of this book. As highlighted in the next section, plea bargaining has become a primary way to resolve disputes in criminal law in Canada.

It is obvious to any casual observer of criminal court proceedings that negotiation is widely used in both Canada and the United States. However, there are no definitive numbers available to demonstrate its prevalence categorically, and there is little systemic research into the ways in which it is carried out. Some of the American research in this area suggests that most criminal convictions occur because of guilty pleas, and assumes that some kind of resolution discussion precedes most convictions (Bibas, 2466, n 9). There is no reason to think that these general features of the criminal justice system in the US are much different in Canada.

As a result, virtually everyone involved in resolving criminal proceedings will spend much of their time seeking to manage disputes through bargaining. This includes lawyers, defence counsel and crown attorneys, paralegals, and other professionals in the justice system. Bargaining can occur in a wide range of specific situations that include charge, procedure, and sentencing discussions. For example:

Bargaining about charges can include:

- Reduction of a charge to a lesser or included offence;[1]
- Withdrawing a charge or staying others;

- Agreement not to proceed on a charge;
- Agreement to withdraw charges as against third parties;
- Agreement to reduce multiple charges to one all-inclusive charge; and
- Agreement to stay certain counts and proceed on others.

Bargaining about procedure can include:

- Agreement to proceed summarily instead of by indictment; [2]
- Agreement to dispose of a case at a particular time if the accused is prepared to waive right to a trial within a reasonable time;[3] and
- Agreement to transfer charges as between jurisdictions.

Bargaining about sentencing can include:

- Recommendations on sentence;
- Crown agreements not to oppose defence sentence recommendations and not to seek optional sanctions;
- Crown agreement not to seek more severe punishments; and
- Types of things in a conditional sentence, such as continued employment or school attendance.

Plea bargaining can occur in both formal and informal settings. Formally, the value of resolution discussions has been entrenched by explicit incorporation into recognized criminal law procedural rules in most jurisdictions. While the specific procedures differ by location, most places provide for supervised judicial pre-trials or pre-trial conferences. These proceedings are regarded as an important mechanism for fairly disposing of criminal matters, or to narrow issues in disputes in the expectation this will expedite litigation. Some Crown policy may support the initiative of individual prosecutors to start such proceedings, as at the federal level where prosecutors are also encouraged to "take whatever steps are reasonably necessary to ensure that such conferences run smoothly" (PPSC, *Deskbook*, s 3.7.5).

However, the ubiquity of negotiation and plea bargaining throughout the Canadian criminal justice system means that much of it occurs informally, beyond the immediate oversight of adjudicative officials (Bibas).

This includes its potential use by child and youth workers, corrections officials, social workers, police and other law enforcement officials, and self-represented litigants. In the case of its most commonly recognized use, the plea bargain, it's also worth noting that there are no technical requirements for counsel to advise the Court that a plea-bargaining arrangement has been made. In practice, where, for example a plea agreement on sentence has been reached, counsel will generally advise a Court that a submission is being made jointly. This notification signals the Court that a plea agreement has likely taken place. For their part, Courts have inherent discretion to supervise proceedings before them, and so have the authority to accept or reject plea agreements. In the case of a joint submission as in the previous example, a Court has jurisdiction to override the agreement between counsel reached through plea bargaining, though in practice a judge would generally accept it on sentence, unless doing so would bring the administration of justice into disrepute.[4]

Research in a wide range of fields has shown that entering plea discussions, or any kind of negotiation process, prepared with a plan grounded in a theorized framework can increase the likelihood that parties will achieve better outcomes. In all cases, it is advisable to have a strategy that includes preparing a specific plan identifying options, as well as steps and techniques to achieve goals and desired outcomes in all kinds of negotiations (Schneider). However, in contexts where no neutral party is supervising the negotiation and acting as a referee, it is particularly important to approach bargaining in an organized fashion.

In short, negotiation and bargaining can take different forms and is a technique used by various different participants in criminal justice, at different stages. It can be overt or implied. The typical bargaining process in criminal law is probably a plea arrangement, which occurs as the result of a discussion between a Crown attorney and defence counsel. However, in some instances resolutions may also occur directly between the prosecution and the accused party, for example, of what the Crown may be prepared to do to reduce charges. The variety of possible negotiations along with the range of circumstances in which resolution discussions can occur means that it's especially important for all advocates working in criminal justice to maintain a high standard of behaviour to ensure fairness and integrity of the process, as well as personal compliance with ethical and professional obligations, all to best protect the interests of clients.

The specific intersection between negotiation and obligations in legal ethics are a focus in Chapter 2. However, in the context of the following scenario, as a general matter, consider what the articling student might do to ensure she is competent and renders an acceptable quality of service that can best help her client with the social and legal challenge that he faces.

NEGOTIATION SCENARIO: Suraida and Bob

Suraida is an articling student for a small firm in a big Canadian city who has been given carriage of a criminal file by her principal, a defence lawyer. The file is a minor charge against Bob, a 37-year-old man, for being drunk and disorderly in public in contravention of s 175(1) (a) (ii) of the *Criminal Code*. On the night in question, at 11:00 PM, Bob was stopped by police as he staggered down the sidewalk along Main Street. When stopped and asked questions by police, Bob replied with slurred speech. When Suraida met with Bob, he told her he had a job working as a labourer doing landscaping ever since he had come to the city from his reserve in Northern Ontario a few years previously. He moved south to care for his 55-year-old father, who suffers from Huntington's disease.

Suraida tells Bob that she knows of the reserve by name, since it is also the home of one of her family members, an adopted cousin. This personal connection appears to relax the client, who tells Suraida that he has a previous conviction for disorderly conduct, and also one for driving while impaired, both many years previously when he was up north. Bob insists that he had only had one beer with a friend on the night he was charged. Bob also says he is afraid that he has inherited the Huntington's gene and has the ailment, a brain disease that has symptoms

Continued

that can be mistaken for intoxication. He tells Suraida he has been too anxious to go to the doctor to find out for sure. Suraida has set a resolution meeting with the Crown Attorney's office early tomorrow morning to discuss the charge.

Discussion Questions

1. If you were Suraida, how might you approach this conversation with the Crown Attorney?
2. What kind of preparations would a competent lawyer or paralegal undertake to ensure they were in the best position to advocate on behalf of Bob?[5]
3. What further actions should Suraida take before she discusses resolution with the Crown?[6]

Make a list addressing these issues, or others you think might be important. As you continue into the next section, compare the preliminary list you have crafted with the organized elements suggested by the model of principled negotiation.

NEGOTIATION: IN THEORY

As a type of "conversation," negotiation is a particular version of conflict resolution. For a negotiation to be effective, the circumstances presuppose that the parties can or must agree on at least some aspects of the dispute, including possible steps in the proceeding and the potential for resolution. Negotiation occurs where parties with interests explore the possibility for agreement on some of these issues, often to avoid, but also as a precursor to, formal adversarial litigation in open court. As noted previously, at their most functional, these agreements can fairly resolve matters quickly and with reduced cost to the client and the administration of justice as a whole. Even where not completely resolved, plea-bargain agreements can advance the proceedings and expedite the legal process.

When lawyers and legal services professionals working in the criminal law sector negotiate, they are engaging in a process that is essentially similar to the kinds of conflict resolutions that are common across many fields. It is important to attend to contextual differences and potential limitations of different bargaining approaches in criminal law. However, overall, legal services professionals need not reinvent the wheel to come up with frameworks for negotiating in criminal law. Rather, legal services professionals can build on the learning available from a widening field of academic study devoted to negotiation theory and practice. This includes a broad range of professionals working in conflict management, but also others in economics, international relations, and psychology, all of whom who have produced a growing, interdisciplinary body of literature on negotiation.

Many writers have theorized about negotiation: some have described it, others have suggested prescriptions for success, and still others have focused on its ethical dimensions. For example, psychologists and other social scientists have theorized about how human minds and social dynamics function, and how these functions can be used to advantage in negotiations (Hollander-Blumhoff, "Social Psychology"). As a further example, ethicists and philosophers have been more typically focused on the ethics of negotiation, often concerning themselves with issues of deception and "bad faith" (Galin), but also considering the ethical risks in negotiation. While we emphasize interest-based negotiation, bargainers face all kinds of different styles and strategies, so it is important to know how to recognize and address them (Roloff, Putnam, and Anastasiou).

The next chapter of this book looks at specific bargaining strategies, including techniques or tactics (Howieson, 10–11), some of which are drawn from the social psychological perspective (Putnam and Powers). Chapter 2 also takes a closer look at the professional obligations of negotiators, as well as further ethical concerns in the criminal context.

In traditional distributive frameworks, negotiation is understood as a form of bargaining, in which both or multiple parties compete adversarially to pitch out positions until they are able to agree on something that is mutually acceptable, often as a way to allocate pieces of a "fixed pie." In this formulation, negotiation can be likened to a combative game (MacFarlane). The major alternative to distributive approaches, which seeks instead to integrate the perspectives of the parties, is "interest-based" negotiation (Fisher and Ury).

In interest-based negotiation, the interaction is reframed from the model of combative game to a form of collaborative problem solving. Some of the desired products include an improved relationship and long-term trust between the parties. Instead of allocating pieces of a "fixed pie," this approach seeks to create value by, for example, expanding the range of options on resolution. In a sense, to carry the analogy forward, the parties end up baking more pie instead of just dividing up the one they already have.

This frame of negotiation tasks each party with ascertaining what the other's underlying interests are, so that both parties then look at the problem together to brainstorm multiple ways in which a dispute can be resolved. This process ideally facilitates a "win-win" solution, through which both are better off than they would have been with a compromise, or with one party winning and the other losing. The goal of an interest-based negotiation is to produce an agreement that:

- represents a **wise** agreement and results in an agreement only if it is possible for the parties to protect their interests;
- has been conducted **efficiently**; and
- fosters a strong **relationship** between the parties, where both the process of the negotiation and the agreement that results improve or at least do not damage the relationship between the parties involved.

In principled negotiation, Fisher and Ury encourage parties to be mindful of the connections between the substance of the negotiation (that is, what is being discussed) and the procedure of the negotiation (that is, how the discussion takes place). Principled negotiation seeks to focus attention on the objective *merits* of a situation. This form of integrative bargaining involves: analysis of the problems faced by each, to arrive at a better understanding of the problem; preparation for the negotiation in a systematic way; and an organized and strategic process for addressing the problem.

Adopting the methodology of principled negotiation is one way that all criminal lawyers and other legal professionals can serve clients better by creating an opportunity for enhanced outcomes in the bargaining process. In general, the first step in this framework is to separate the people from the substance of the dispute by taking steps to focus on the dimensions of the problem itself. This is done by first focusing on the parties' interests, rather than on the positions they may advance. Then, the parties are encouraged to consider as many options as can be conceived for resolution, by generating a variety of alternatives before deciding what to do. The method also involves a refocusing of both parties' attention on objective criteria to assess ways in which the parties' interests are addressed by the options considered. The specific steps to begin thinking about a principled negotiation are set out and discussed in further detail in the next section.

THE "SEVEN ELEMENTS" OF PRINCIPLED BARGAINING

Negotiators can use structured preparation through an organized bargaining plan to effectively and efficiently achieve their strategic ends. In our own work, and in thinking about integrative bargaining in criminal law, we find it helpful to use the "Seven Elements" approach (Fisher and Ury) as a model to prepare for negotiation. The Seven Elements are as follows:

1. Interests

A first step in preparing for negotiation is to consider the interests of each party. A key point in this approach is that interests diverge from positions. Interests are what a party values or needs. In contrast, positions are the statements parties make that announce what they say they want to achieve in a negotiation. As a criminal law proceeding, the interests of the party will inevitably include legal considerations, such as defence requests to consider particular sentencing recommendations.

However, the interests of an accused in such circumstances may include other considerations beyond strictly legal factors.

In the case of the hypothetical scenario, interests to be identified by the articling student will include concern about conviction and sentencing on the charge. Consider our negotiation case study again. Bob has already suggested in his interview with Suraida several other potential interests that may be just as important to him. For example, Bob's family responsibilities as a caretaker and his work may mean he wishes to resolve the criminal litigation in as minimally intrusive a way as possible. Bob's health situation may also be a factor, both as information that could be helpful in addressing the charge, but also in terms of his personal well-being. Last, Bob's previous residence on a reserve suggests he may be Indigenous, which could be a factor subject to distinct procedures under the *Criminal Code* (s 718.1 (e)).

To first develop an approach identifying interests, it's important to consider the other party's interests as well. Considerations and special duties of the Crown are a further subject of discussion in the next chapter, but for now it's enough to know that the prosecution's main duty is to enforce the law, but to do so in the public interest.[7] "Interests" are the reasons behind positions taken by either side in bargaining, and may not be readily apparent as they are often submerged, sometimes behind the competitive position and posturing of those who adopt distributive strategies. A singular concern for legalities in criminal law may mean that either party in negotiations may not have fully thought through, or be able to articulate, the interests underlying their positions, so it is good practice to consider these in advance, and from all sides.

As a best practice to understand your own interests, try to be radically honest with yourself. What values or needs are in play when you enter any given negotiation? Then try to put yourself in your counterpart's shoes. What brings them to this conversation with you? What could they hope to gain from an agreement? Write these interests down in a checklist to ensure you have adequately explored all potential implications.

Since specific interests are sometimes not obvious, it is useful to explore and deconstruct them before the negotiation begins. Here, professional advocates who take on negotiations also need to think specifically in terms of potential conflicts of interest. For some legal professionals like counsel, this is a legal duty defined in the Federation of Law Societies' *Model Code*:

> A "**conflict of interest**" means the existence of a substantial risk that a lawyer's loyalty to or representation of a client would be materially and adversely affected by the lawyer's own interest or the lawyer's duties to another client, a former client, or a third person. (FLSC, *Model Code*, "Definitions")

For lawyers in Canada, the regulatory duty involving conflicts requires them not just to not be in a conflict, but to take proactive steps to *avoid* them as well (FLSC, *Model Code*, s 3.4). It appears in the hypothetical case of Suraida and Bob that the articling student may have a personal connection to the client's home reserve. While such facts may appear innocuous, and may not rise to the level of a disqualifying conflict, her positive duty in law means that Suraida would be best advised to inquire further, to clarify her family connection, and to ensure that she did not have a personal interest conflict.

In seeking to identify the other side's interests in any bargaining situation, some of them also arise from the circumstances of the case and may seem obvious. However, it's a good practice to start resolution discussions by asking some open-ended questions, to explore and confirm the interests at stake. Here, developing a better understanding of the underlying interests of the prosecution is "critical to an integrative bargaining approach" (Roberts and Wright, 1487).

After you develop a list of interests, circle the interests you and your counterpart have in common. Plan to explore and highlight your shared interests as the negotiation progresses: creating a sense of mutual understanding can help re-orient the parties away from conflict and towards a common endeavour. Exploring and understanding interests can also facilitate better lines of communication. Ultimately, you should assess whether you are able to arrive at a good agreement based on whether its terms fulfill interests, not whether the parties have successfully achieved whatever objectives they may have first articulated in their positions.

2. Options

Exploring options, both before the negotiation and as a step towards a more collaborative conversation during the negotiation, is a way to create value and help fulfill shared interests. As a first step in developing options, a best practice is to develop alternatives through a process of brainstorming, an activity in which a large quantity of possible ideas is put forward without judgement.

In brainstorming, it's important to take note of a number of possible options before exploring or settling on any. For instance, in negotiating sentence, not every deal needs to involve just an agreement as to the duration of a sentence. Looking at a wider range of sentencing options, such as asking for restorative steps to be taken or restitution to be made, can be a way expand the options available for resolution. In addition to legal considerations related to Bob's potential Indigenous status, his past convictions beg questions about whether he might have suffered or continue to suffer from substance abuse problems, which might be amenable to treatment. Similarly, to the extent he could have a genetic ailment, Bob's diagnosis and treatment might also be a factor that could be considered (Freckleton).

A useful next step in preparing for negotiation is to consider the practicalities of the various options that might be available for an agreement. Very often, parties are focused too narrowly on one single solution and, as a result, do not see other paths forward. This often comes from premature judgement in relation to outcomes, and is sometimes based on a failure to systematically prepare for negotiations. The failure to plan can have a substantial effect on the perceived credibility and legitimacy of the negotiators, which is the next element considered.

3. Legitimacy

In advance of the negotiation, as well as through the course of the interaction, consider carefully and critically how you determine which options for resolution are legitimate. Decide what objective criteria or standards are legally and ethically applicable, or create a sense of fairness in the matter. In the criminal law context, legitimacy will in part be measured by the ranges of discretion made available in the legislation and what guidance is provided by case law.

A big part of establishing both credibility and legitimacy lies in preparation. For instance, if there is a mandatory minimum sentence set out in the *Criminal Code*, any option for agreement that falls outside of that range may be regarded as an illegitimate non-starter. Alternatively, providing the facts, research, and legal reasoning to support objective criteria provides a basis to determine if a particular option has objective legitimacy (Oliver and Batra, 68–70).

Preparatory tasks as part of developing options might also include investigating the scene of the offence, interviewing potential witnesses, conducting legal research, or developing a theory of the case (Roberts and Wright, 1480–82). In fact, studies suggest that defence counsel often fail to do even the most basic preparation in developing bargaining options (Doyel, 1025–27).

In considering the hypothetical involving Suraida and Bob, for example, it's possible that the evenness of the sidewalk or lighting in the location where Bob was stopped affected his sense of balance, so examining the location where the alleged offence took place might be a good idea. The facts presented also suggest there is a further witness, Bob's friend, who if interviewed in advance might be able to confirm how much alcohol Bob actually consumed before he was charged.[8] If Bob's personal fears are realized and he is suffering from Huntington's disease, Suraida might also investigate how courts have previously dealt with such factors, which might in turn provide a basis for a legal defence in the case. Considering the legitimacy of possible options for agreement is a crucial way to establish credibility in examining negotiation alternatives.

4. Alternatives to Agreement

Another consideration that negotiators should always bear in mind are the alternatives to an agreement. Negotiators should understand their best alternative to a negotiated agreement (BATNA) so that they do not settle for agreements that leave their interests less well protected than a situation where no agreement was achieved. For instance, counsel should generally not agree to a joint submission on sentencing that represents a worse outcome with reference to their interests than is likely to transpire if a judge rules on the matter. This point may seem somewhat obvious, but it is useful to take a step back and systematically look at the range of possible outcomes.

It is empowering to have a clear sense of a backup plan or plan B, based on the BATNA. Negotiators should not only work to understand their BATNA but also strive to improve upon it. Knowing when you can abandon negotiations if your client's interests aren't being met helps negotiators determine what value an agreement creates and to assess whether it is a good bargain for their side.

In the criminal context, calculating a BATNA may be more complex than in other settings. First, limited resources and high workloads of duty counsel, for example, along with the reality in some cases that there may be no real defence to a particular charge, means that the only alternative to an agreement is the threat of going to trial (Roberts and Wright, 1472). A second factor in situations where alternatives appear limited is that failure to agree at an early stage may seem to leave a criminal trial as the only option. But as the prospect of a trial becomes more realized over time, the desire to avoid costly and involved litigation, especially if it concerns relatively minor criminal offences, may precipitate further resolution discussions at a later stage (Roberts, 1089).

5. Communication

Clear, intentional communication is crucial for effective negotiation. Perception and understanding are foundational to re-orienting towards a common goal, one of the primary objectives of interest-based negotiation. The types of adversarial and persuasive communication lawyers are often taught as advocates are generally not what is required. Interest-based negotiation requires lawyers bargaining in the criminal proceedings to do quite the opposite of what most legal professionals are trained to do in formal oral presentations arguing a case.

In advocacy, for example, one thing we are taught is to control the interaction of questioning witnesses and to ask questions calculated to produce anticipated answers. However, when negotiating, we are tasked with listening more than talking; we need to ask questions, similar to the way a researcher or journalist might ask them to gather information. To the extent that a bargainer does talk and potentially reveal information about their clients or the situation, they should do so based on a plan about what to disclose, in a structured and strategic exchange of information (Roberts and Wright, 1487).

We need to be curious; we need to ask questions for which we do not know the answers. In preparing for a negotiation, counsel should plan to ask about the other side's interests. We should ask about their range of alternatives. Before going into the negotiation, it is a good idea to write out a list of questions that we need to ask. After planning how to listen in communication, we should also plan our most effective method to explain our client's interests. Part of this process is to assess how to communicate to the other party that some interests, at least, are shared. In the case of Suraida and Bob, the prosecution will have to consider a number of things that include the cost of pursuing a relatively minor charge, the possibility of a successful defence, and the reasonable prospect of conviction (*Henry*, para 61). In this instance, effective communications to advocate on Bob's behalf early in negotiation could facilitate a mutually beneficial and expedited resolution.

The following are some further overall tips identified by Fisher and Ury that can also help ensure the parties have constructive patterns of communication:

- Engage in active listening, focusing on what the counterpart is saying and not jumping to your next statement;
- Acknowledge and restate what has been said for clarification and affirmation;
- Speak in a way that is mindful of your audience; use language that is likely to be understood by the counterpart;
- Speak about yourself, not about the other party: describe a problem in terms of its impact on you ("I feel disappointed" or "I am put at risk by this" instead of "you betrayed my confidence and I can't trust your word"); and
- Prepare so that you communicate with purpose.

6. Relationship

One important element of integrative bargaining focuses on the significance of relations. Some limitations to integrative bargaining might arise in situations where there is only one issue in a limited negotiation, but even these potential constraints may be mitigated by the collegial nature of criminal law practice over time. When we view court cases through the lens of our personal lives, or via television or cinematic entertainment, the story arc and outcome of the case is very significant. It is true that our cases matter, but they are not our careers, and ongoing relationships are likely to be a more significant factor in our capacity to effectively represent the interests of clients than the outcome of any one negotiation.

Years of practice and involvement in criminal law have underscored to us the extent to which it is important to establish and attend to individual reputational concerns related to interactions with others in order to be an effective negotiator. As an articling student, Suraida has only just begun to establish her professional reputation. Over the course of our careers, as professionals advocating for the best interests of clients in criminal law matters, it is very likely that we will run into the same judges, lawyers, paralegals, and other court officials on the other side time and time again, so it's important to develop a reputation for diligence, conscientiousness, and integrity (FLSC, *Model Code*, s 2).

Consequently, the productive relationships we develop with our professional colleagues in law are very important. Principled negotiation is intended to re-orient the parties to understand themselves not always as adversarially opposing each other but sometimes as standing side by side, confronting a problem together. We must always strive to balance our interest in a good agreement or decision in a case, and our duties to clients, with our ongoing collegial and professional obligations and interests in working constructively with one another. In turn, we must balance these obligations with the interests of justice.[9]

Making relationships a priority does not mean that we should not explore areas of conflict. Some relationships may appear harmonious when they are in fact full of latent, unexpressed conflict. On this point, it is important to be direct and clear in communicating, and, as Fisher and Ury admonish negotiators, not to simply give in to the other party in order to avoid a fight. They recommend optimizing transparency, engaging in active listening, and cultivating empathy in negotiations. Some further discussion of specific communications tactics to build rapport and enhance relational interactions in negotiations are contained in Chapter 2.

7. Commitment

Legal advocates know that commitment is a vital part of the overall duty of loyalty lawyers owe to clients (FLSC, *Model Code*, s 3.4-1, Commentary [5]). It is vital that negotiators understand their own scope of authority to make an agreement and that of their counterparts, but to also remember that the primary duty is always to those they represent. This obligation is incorporated directly into the lawyer professional rules addressing plea agreements, which acknowledge and expressly permit disposition discussions "unless the client instructs otherwise" (FLSC, *Model Code*, 5.1-7). Defence lawyers are also explicitly directed to ensure their clients have been advised about the prospects for acquittal, the implications and possible consequences of a guilty plea, the authority of the court, and that the accused must be prepared to admit the necessary factual and mental elements of an offence. Last, a lawyer can only enter into an agreement about a guilty plea if they have been voluntarily instructed to do so by their client (FLSC, *Model Code*, s 5.1-8).

One practical consideration in integrative bargaining is to ensure commitment to agreements. Some simple steps can help clarify expectations and lessen the likelihood that terms of any agreement might later be in dispute. For example, it is useful to reduce commitments in a negotiation to writing so they can be included in a final agreement, which the parties can confirm by signing off. Commitments should include any implementation issues or conditions. In the case of Suraida and Bob, if the Crown was willing for example to dismiss charges based on a medical diagnosis of Huntington's, what would happen if this was not forthcoming?

Commitments should also include a timeline that is linked to any critical steps that might be necessary to implement the arrangement.

Last, lawyers should always remember that in making interim arrangements in a matter to do something, which may not always initially be in writing, any undertakings given are considered the personal promise and responsibility of counsel (FLSC, *Model Code,* s 5.16 and 7.2-11).

POTENTIAL LIMITATIONS OF PRINCIPLED BARGAINING

While we focus on principled negotiation as an approach in criminal law, this perspective has some potential limitations. One issue is that either side in a negotiation may use a different approach, or techniques and tactics that reflect a more competitive strategy. In addition to being aware of some potential limitations, it's important for all bargainers to be able to recognize when other parties may be using different, particular distributive approaches (Lande), to understand why, how, and when interest-based approaches are more likely to succeed.

Interest-based bargaining presumes the potential for agreement on objective criteria to determine the underlying merit. In the justice system, the underlying criteria might well involve disputes over issues with which there is legitimate disagreement, leading to conflicting characterizations of legitimacy of the positions advanced (Oliver and Batra). Such things might include disputes over the applicability of case law (FLSC, *Model Code*, 3.2-7 (e), 5.1-2 (b), (i), (e)), or relevance of evidence and witnesses.

For example, a long-established obligation of the Crown in Canadian law is to call all credible material witnesses. However, the determination of whom may fit this category is largely within the control of the prosecution, which may or may not accept the legitimacy of aspects of whatever theory of the case has been developed by the defence. Where the defence could not effectively assert the material credibility of a prospective witness, the fairness of a subsequent Crown refusal to call them might have to be one of the "legitimate differences of opinion," which in law sometimes can only be determined by a judge (*R v Hillis*). In such cases, integrative tactics may have to yield to acknowledge the adversarial imperatives of the legal system, and the duty of both defence and Crown counsel is to act in all cases "resolutely" for their clients (FLSC, *Model Code*, 5.1-1, 5.1-3).

As another example, some note that where bargaining is restricted to considering only one or a small number of critical issues, the opportunity to develop relational communications, or a range of optional outcomes, may be more constrained. In such cases, positional tactics developed in traditional bargaining contexts may be a better way to proceed (Fisher). However, even in these kinds of situations in criminal law, small populations of professionals working to resolve criminal disputes increases the prospect of longer-term professional interactions and relations, which in turn may enhance the openness to integrative approaches over time (Menkel-Meadow, 785–787).

Ultimately, there may be some limited situations, like those set out above, where distributive or other tactics can be used effectively. Bargainers should be prepared to recognize and deal with these other approaches. However, in our view, the prevalence of bargaining as a dominant process in criminal justice means that over-reliance on competitive approaches is ill-advised. More generally widespread adoption of distributive approaches in criminal law would likely lead to considerable systemic dysfunction (Roberts and Wright, 1474, n 101). With these possible qualifications in mind, we turn now to discuss the individual "style" that people bring to the bargaining table, and how it can enhance negotiations.

LEVERAGING YOUR NEGOTIATING STYLE

In this section, we distinguish between the overall method of principled negotiation, and individual "style" or personal behaviours in bargaining. Everyone has different personalities that are integrated, through nature, training, and experience, into our own professional personas. Part of the methodology of principled negotiation is a framework for leveraging these individual negotiating styles. In preparing for bargaining, it is useful to separate the people from the problem, not to ignore that there are people with personalities and habits involved, but by becoming mindful and attentive to that reality.

For example, all negotiations involve a degree of stress and potential anxiety, which clients might express in different ways. One trick to acknowledge and accommodate the different ways in which people may react in a negotiating context is to allocate sufficient time for parties to let off steam and work through any emotions triggered by bargaining. In fact, there may be some benefit to try to draw out those emotions and to address them at an early stage in the conversation, initially raising the level of conflict rather than lowering it. In some cases, individuals may not even be conscious of their underlying emotional investment in issues being addressed, so allowing them to express in an open way can both improve communications and help to further clarify individual interests.

It is also important to appreciate how individual bargainers can become invested personally with a position taken in negotiation. Lawyers have been trained in advocacy and persuasion, and some may still view success as trying to "win" in adversarial contests. It's important to remember that however invested in the outcome an individual advocate may be, the interests they are representing are first and foremost those of their clients. In this respect, all professional bargainers should keep in mind the professional objectivity encouraged by lawyers' professional conduct rules (FLSC, *Model Code*, 5.1-1, Commentary [5]), which admonish counsel to refrain from expressing personal opinions on the merits of a case, and to absolutely not express subjective views or beliefs with respect to anything that is properly the subject of legal proof (FLSC, *Model Code*, 5.2-1, Commentary [1]).

In any event, from an integrative bargaining perspective, a "win" by the defence on behalf of their clients often involves a wide range of considerations beyond just the legal outcome. For the prosecution, this means that they are also obliged to consider the broader public interest in the administration of justice. In this case, the traditional position in Canadian law is that the Crown does not "win" through victory in the courtroom or at the bargaining table, but through seeing justice done (FLSC, *Model Code*, 5.1-3). However, the individual style and personal desire to be successful that people bring to the table remain important considerations, which need to be examined.

In order to pay attention to the underlying interests motivating the parties in any negotiation, it is important to develop an awareness of our own negotiation styles, but it's also important to be able to identify and respond effectively to the bargaining styles of our counterparts. Various authors have provided typologies for different conflict styles. We find helpful the framework offered by Callum Coburn, as follows:

- Competitive—negotiators who seek to win and simultaneously ensure that the other side loses;
- Accommodating—negotiators who permit the other side to win in the interests of protecting the relationship;
- Avoidant—negotiators who make efforts not to engage in conversations/situations where there is conflict;
- Compromise—negotiators who "split the difference" so that each side gives something up to keep the other satisfied; and
- Collaborative—negotiators who seek to produce a "win-win" by understanding and seeking to address the interests of both parties.

Each style identified above has its advantages and disadvantages. Coburn notes that competitive styles are useful when parties seek to arrive at a result quickly, but are not helpful when parties could benefit from later collaboration with a counterpart. On the other hand, accommodating conflict styles may result in apparent agreements, but can lead to long-term resentment and latent conflict, as well as to agreements to which the accommodating party may not really commit.

Avoidant styles can prevent an agenda from moving forward, but they can also be appropriate when the counterpart is very powerful and there is likely to be some sort of violent or otherwise problematic repercussion to a confrontation. At the same time, compromise can ensure that both parties gain some advantage from an agreement, but it is likely to result in discontent on the part of both parties. Compromise can be problematic from the perspective of interest-based negotiation, because it fails to create new value. In an interest-based framework, collaboration is the preferred style, as it allows for value creation and mutual problem-solving, and works most effectively when both sides are buying into the method.

SUMMARY

This chapter has provided an overview of negotiation in the criminal context. It started by exploring common circumstances in which criminal lawyers and professionals providing legal services in the criminal milieu engage in negotiation, stressing that negotiations are frequent and significant in the work of criminal lawyers. We introduced a basic example of a potential negotiation in the imagined case of Suraida and Bob. This scenario dealt with a legal professional's consideration of a possible resolution discussion with the Crown of a minor criminal charge. We then provided a brief overview and explication of common theories about and methodologies for negotiation, focusing particularly on integrative or "interest-based" negotiation. Our description of the application of Fisher and Ury's Seven Elements in this area was illustrated by reference to our earlier hypothetical. We also acknowledged and addressed some potential limits to integrative bargaining in criminal law. This chapter concluded by distinguishing overall approach from style, and briefly discussed the importance of stylistic adaptations negotiators can benefit from using. The next chapter looks more closely at negotiation in the criminal context, the special role of the Crown, and the competencies of negotiation, including the capacity to use an interest-based approach, combined with individual style to strategize and plan for specific negotiations.

SUGGESTIONS FOR FURTHER READING

Burke, Alafair S. "Improving Prosecutorial Decision Making: Some Lessons in Cognitive Science." (2006) 47 *Wm & Mary L Rev* 1587.

Dickie, Mary Lou. "Through the Looking Glass—Ethical Responsibilities of the Crown in Resolution Discussion in Ontario." (2005) 50 *Crim LQ* 128, at 147.

EASYPol. 2008. "Negotiation Theory and Practice." <http://www.fao.org/docs/up/easypol/550/4-5_negotiation_background_paper_179en.pdf>.

Pitel, S.G.A., and Y.S. Gadsden-Chung. "Reconsidering a Lawyer's Obligation to Raise Adverse Authority." (2016) 49 *UBCL Rev* 521.

Program on Negotiation at Harvard Law School. <www.pon.harvard.edu>.

Quicksprout. "A Step-by-Step Guide to Winning (Almost) Every Single Negotiation." 2012. <http://www.quicksprout.com/2012/02/02/a-step-by-step-guide-to-winning-almost-every-single-negotiation/>.

Thompson, Leigh. *Negotiation Theory and Research*. New York: Taylor and Francis, 2006.

Uphoff, Rodney J. "The Criminal Defence Lawyer as Effective Negotiator: A Systemic Approach." (1995) 3 *Clinical L Rev* 73.

Wetlaufer, Gerald B. "The Limits of Integrative Bargaining." (1997) 85 *Geo L J* 369.

Women's Institute of Negotiation. "Negotiating Style Self-Assessment." 2011. <http://womennegotiationinstitute.com/doc/WIN_Negotiation_Style_Assessment_0711.pdf>.

ENDNOTES

1. See *R v Beyo*; under s 606 (4) of the *Criminal Code*, this includes an offence arising out of the same transaction.

2. Some criminal offences are "hybrid" in Canada, where the Crown can elect either summary, or more serious indictable procedures; see *R v Dudley*.

3. S 11(b) of the *Charter of Rights* provides that any person has the right to be tried for an offence within a reasonable time. "Reasonableness" in this context has been the subject of considerable jurisprudential consideration; see *R v Jordan*.

4. See *R v Anthony-Cook*; a finding of "abuse of process" may also bring the administration of justice into disrepute (*R v Babos*); see also *R v Dorsey*.

5. Though not yet "called to the Bar," as an articling student, Suraida is generally subject to professional lawyer rules directly. Her lawyer principal also takes responsibility for her actions; see FLSC, *Model Code* Definitions, "lawyer" and s 6.2-2 and Commentary at [1].

6. See consideration of Huntington's disease as a factor in Canadian criminal law in *R v Belcourt*.

7. See *Boucher v The Queen* [1955] SCR 16.

8. In this case, Suraida would also want to review her professional obligations when communicating with witnesses, described in the FLSC, *Model Code*, s 5.4.

9. Addressing plea agreements, the Commentary to FLSC, *Model Code* notes, "the public interest in the proper administration of justice should not be sacrificed in the interest of expediency" at s 5.1-8 [1].

REFERENCES

Bibas, Stephanos. "Plea Bargaining Outside the Shadow of the Trial." (2004) 117 *Harv L Rev* 2463.

Boucher v The Queen [1955] SCR 16.

Canadian Charter of Rights and Freedoms, Schedule B, *Constitution Act 1982*, Part I [*Charter* or *Charter of Rights*].

Coburn, Callum. *Negotiation Conflict Styles.* Boston: Harvard University Press, 2015.

Condlin, Robert J. "Bargaining Without Law." (2012) 56 *NYL Sch L Rev* 281.

Criminal Code of Canada RSC 1985, c, C-46 [*Criminal Code*].

Doyel, Robert L. "The National College-Mercer Criminal Defence Survey: Some Preliminary Observations about Interview, Counselling, and Plea Negotiations." (1986) 37 *Mercer L Rev* 1019.

Federation of Law Societies. *Model Code of Professional Conduct* [FLSC, *Model Code*], as amended March 14, 2017. <https://flsc.ca/wp-content/uploads/2018/03/Model-Code-as-amended-March-2017-Final.pdf>. Accessed January 20, 2019.

Fisher, Roger. "Negotiating Power." (1983) 27 *American Behavioural Scientist* 123.

Fisher, Roger, and William Ury. *Getting to Yes: Negotiating Agreement without Giving in*, 3rd ed. Harmondsworth, UK: Penguin, 2011.

Freckleton, Ian. "Huntington's Disease and the Law." (2010) 18 *Journal of Law and Medicine* 7–18.

Galin, Amira. *The World of Negotiation: Theories, Perceptions, and Practice.* Tel Aviv: World Scientific, 2015.

Henry v British Columbia (AG), [2015] SCJ No 24, 2015 SCC 24.

Hollander-Blumhoff, Rebecca. Note. "Getting to Guilty: Plea Bargaining as Negotiation." (1997) 2 *Harv Negot L Rev* 115.

Hollander-Blumhoff, Rebecca. "Social Psychology, Information Processing, and Plea Bargaining." (2007) 91 *Marq L Rev* 163.

Howieson, Jill. *Negotiation: Strategy, Styles, Skills*, 2nd ed. Toronto: LexisNexis Butterworths, 2010.

Lande, John. "Taming the Jungle of Negotiation Theories." 2017. University of Missouri School of Law Legal Studies Research Paper. <https://papers.ssrn.com/sol3/papers.cfm?abstract_id=3089855>. Accessed January 20, 2019.

MacFarlane, Julie. *Dispute Resolution Readings and Case Studies*, 3rd ed. Toronto: Emond Montgomery Publications, 2011.

Menkel-Meadow, Carrie. "Toward Another View of Legal Negotiation: The Structure of Problem Solving." (1984) 31 *UCLA L Rev* 754.

Oliver, Wesley MacNeil, and Rishi Batra. "Standards of Legitimacy in Criminal Negotiations." (2015) 20 *Harv Negot L R* 61.

Public Prosecution Service of Canada. *Deskbook* [PPSC, *Deskbook*]. <https://www.ppsc-sppc.gc.ca/eng/pub/fpsd-sfpg/fps-sfp/tpd/p3/ch07.html>. Accessed January 20, 2019.

Putnam, Linda L., and Samantha Rae Powers. "Developing Negotiating Competencies," in Angret F. Hannawa and Brian Spitzberg, editors, *Communication Competencies*. Berlin: De Gruyter Mouton, 2015.

R v Anthony-Cook, 2016 SCC 43 CanLII.

R v Babos, 2014 SCC 16 CanLII.

R v Belcourt, 2000 441 BCCA CanLII.

R v Beyo, 2000 5683 (OCA) CanLII.

R v Dorsey, 43 WCB (2d) 273, (1999) 123 O.A.C. 342 (OCA).

R v Dudley, 2009 SCC 58 CanLII.

R v Hillis, 2016 ONSC 451 CanLII.

R v Jordan, 2016 SCC 27 CanLII.

Roberts, Jenny. "Crashing the Misdemeanour System." (2013) 70 *Wash & Lee L Rev* 1089.

Roberts, Jenny, and Ronald F. Wright. "Training for Bargaining." (2016) 57 *Wm & Mary L Rev* 1445.

Roloff, Michael E., Linda L. Putnam, and Lefki Anastasiou. "Negotiation Skills," in John O. Green and Brant R. Burleson, editors, *Handbook of Communication and Social Interaction Skills*. Mahwah, NJ: Lawrence Erlbaum Associates, 2003.

Schneider, Andrea Kupfer. "Shattering Negotiation Myths: Empirical Evidence on the Effectiveness of Negotiation Style." (2002) 7 *Harv Negot L Rev* 143.

CHAPTER 2

Conflict Resolution: Theory and Practice, Competence, Ethics, Strategies, and Tactics in Criminal Law Negotiations

LEARNING OBJECTIVES

After reading this chapter, students should:

- Have familiarity with conflict resolution theory and its application in criminal law
- Know negotiation competencies in criminal law bargaining
- Understand the ethical implications of criminal law bargaining in Canada
- Develop insight into conflict styles and appreciate the need to modify personal style to fit circumstances
- Understand strategies and specific techniques for de-escalating, managing, and resolving conflicts in criminal negotiations

OVERVIEW

The criminal justice system is set up to provide a framework for addressing a particular genre of conflicts: where individuals or entities violate criminal prohibitions and thereby come into conflict with the state. To a large extent, conflict is an unavoidable and natural part of the human experience, and criminal law provides one system to resolve these kinds of disputes. In criminal proceedings, ancillary conflicts can also develop between people working in the administration of justice. Legal professionals often face additional challenges caused by the stresses, busy-ness, heavy workload, and strains of their jobs.

This chapter sets out some theoretical perspectives on conflict resolution, before contextualizing some of the particular challenges negotiators face in criminal law. It also examines the important and distinct legal ethical obligations in this setting, and presents a hypothetical to illustrate some of these ethical issues. One of these challenges is the question of "civility" in law and in communications, which is also highlighted by examining a case study, to provide a departure point for further discussion.

The chapter subsequently focuses on strategies for practitioners to de-escalate, manage, and resolve conflicts that arise in the course of their work. These include managing emotions, effective communications, and acknowledging the influence of conflict styles and adapting them to the circumstances while focusing on mindful collaboration. Within these strategies, we identify and discuss specific ethical, emotional, and cognitive pitfalls that all negotiators should avoid. We also suggest several techniques and tips to enhance collaborative negotiation skills as they are employed in criminal proceedings. These strategies and specific tactics can help to address alternate approaches and also enhance the opportunity for interest-based bargaining to improve outcomes in criminal law bargaining.

CONFLICT RESOLUTION: IN THEORY

The study of how to resolve disputes peacefully has come to be understood as conflict resolution theory. Where conflicts are not resolvable, attention turns instead to managing them effectively. There are a variety of theoretical lenses through which conflict, conflict resolution, and conflict management have been considered across a wide swath of academic disciplines. Historically, research and writing about conflict resolution focused on military confrontations and international relations more generally, along with examinations of labour disputes (Bercovitch *et al*.). Starting a few decades ago, researchers started inquiring into the psychological and social underpinnings of conflict.

From a social perspective, conflicts have been described as following a pattern where they emerge, are then transformed into disputes with legal dimensions, responsibility is ascribed, and remedies pursued (Felstiner and Sarat). From a psychological viewpoint, conflict also has cognitive dimensions based upon what parties think and perceive. These psychosocial approaches may also consider individual emotional factors, relating to how those involved feel or behave in relation to the ways they manage, address, and resolve conflicts (Mayer).

The application of social and psychological perspectives to conflict has supported the differentiation of dispute resolution over the last few years. Approaches that offered alternatives to the formal legal system, including negotiation, mediation, and arbitration, grew in popularity starting in the 1970s (Bercovitch *et al.*). Since then, these alternatives have transformed the settlement of disputes in the legal system (Macfarlane, 7).

Pragmatic approaches to alternative dispute resolution (ADR) are based in certain foundational theories about conflict resolution, which are shared by influential scholars writing in the area (Furlong; Caspersen). These foundational ideas include that conflict:

- Normally arises in human relationships;
- Can be productive when it provides an opportunity for change;
- Does not inescapably have to be understood as a zero-sum competition where the only possible outcomes are winning and losing;
- Is understood in terms of both resolution and management, rooted in communication; and
- Resolution and management also involve emotional components that need to be managed, expressed, and understood.

This environmental scan of conflict resolution theory situates "interest-based" approaches to negotiation in criminal law. Our work in this chapter emphasizes this integrative bargaining approach to focus on behavioural aspects of conflict resolution, suggesting practical strategies for parties and representatives. Additional theoretical perspectives on conflict resolution are included for further reading at the end of this chapter. Next, we turn to consider pragmatic challenges for criminal law negotiators arising from conflict in terms of ethical considerations.

CONFLICT IN THE CRIMINAL CONTEXT

We know from experience and research that virtually all human inter-actions carry the potential for conflict (Porter-O'Grady). In the modern challenge of criminal justice, many professionals face large volumes of work. This heavy workload is often exacerbated by various pressures in-cluding a lack of time and resources, and dealing with difficult individ-ual personalities. What many think of as "criminal justice" in Canada is the result of intersections between multiple systems, organizations, and individuals: adjudication, court, social and correctional services, as well as lawyers, paralegals, law firms, and government counsel. Law en-forcement personnel, such as police, interact with defence lawyers and Crown Attorneys in Canada, along with probation and parole officers.

Within all of these settings, conflict has the potential to be dys-functional and present barriers to problem-solving and fulfilling work. On this point, there has been some study that shows, in Canada, justice system participants face a high risk of being exposed to violence, includ-ing threats and intimidation from the subjects of criminal investiga-tions (Bourdeau, 11–23). Violence against lawyers and law enforcement officers, as well as judges, can be a real risk in Canada as well as in the United States (Brown), and is recognized through the inclusion of a *Criminal Code* provision creating a hybrid offence subject to a penalty of 14 years in jail (s 423.1).

In addition to direct risks, legal professionals deal indirectly with pressure associated with the repercussions of violent criminal acts, which can exacerbate workplace tensions. Along with underlying con-flict inherent in criminal law, interpersonal conflict can also be found in these work settings in the form of bullying, threats, intimidation, and assaults. Over the last few years, Canadians have begun recognizing and responding more generally to these various forms of workplace vio-lence (Bolton and Griffiths).

Perhaps more common in the setting of criminal law negotiations is a situation where an overly competitive bargainer, or their client, es-calates conflict by appearing to make threats in relation to proceed-ings. On this point, and in addition to criminal prohibitions on physical threats, lawyers are prohibited by their regulatory rules from threatening to initiate or proceed with criminal or quasi-criminal charges, and from threatening regulatory proceedings (FLSC, *Model Code*, 3.2-5).

Some interpersonal and workplace conflict is likely inevitable in all human interactions. It's important to acknowledge that, from a broader perspective, conflict is also an inherent part of an adversarial criminal justice system. In this respect, we need to recognize the wide nature of conflict, and to address legal disputes in criminal law negotiations effectively. Consistent professionalism to resolve or reduce the variety of these conflicts is consequently a significant part of the negotiating skills of all legal professionals. As set out next, all negotiators must demonstrate their competence and ethical skills to bargain in criminal proceedings.

COMPETENCE AND PROFESSIONALISM IN NEGOTIATION

Within the broader context of conflict resolution, and the environment of criminal law in Canada, all legal service providers who bargain need to have the requisite skill and knowledge to act effectively on behalf of their clients. There is broad agreement that overall negotiating competencies consist of six common topics (Gadlin *et al.*, 53), introduced in the first chapter, but distinguished further here. Core competencies for all negotiators include the:

1. Idea of personal style, including how it relates to adversarial and "interest-based" bargaining;
2. Place of integrative versus distributive bargaining approaches;
3. Idea of a "bargaining zone" or scope, including the BATNA;
4. Creating of options through activities like brainstorming;
5. Importance of preparation; and
6. Use of listening, talking, and other communications skills.

Some legal professionals are explicitly expected to demonstrate negotiating competencies as part of their regulatory obligations (FLSC, *Model Code*, 3.1-1 (c), (v)). This includes the skills, which are behaviours related to particular criteria or outcomes, but also knowledge and behaviours that influence negotiation performance, including the process, how to manage interactions, and learning how to transform the course of a particular bargaining session (Putnam and Powers, 367–368).

In addition to a general and legal ethical obligation to be competent, legal professionals should always act with "integrity" (FLSC, *Model Code*, 2.1). Some note that this expectation moderates a long tradition of "zealous" advocacy in law and is the principle through which all Canadian legal ethical principles are interpreted (Woolley). The view that unconstrained zealousness in advocacy is inappropriate is reflected in lawyer codes of conduct that now oblige them to act "resolutely" instead (FLSC, *Model Code*, 5.1-1).

As highlighted in Chapter 1, lawyer rules also spell out some important expectations in negotiations. This includes a primary duty of loyalty (FLSC, *Model Code*, s 3.4-1, Commentary [5]), which comprises obligations to be committed to a client, to act to avoid conflicts of interest, to respect confidentiality, and to act with candour in the professional relationship. Specific lawyer duties also highlight the fact that representing clients requires a high degree of confidence and that all negotiators will keep clients informed, advise them of risks, and seek to advance their interests. From a broad perspective, ethical obligations place all bargainers in a position to act as "trusted intermediaries" (Leering), to protect clients and to manage interactions in often very difficult circumstances. In criminal law negotiations, representatives frequently bargain about fundamental rights, involving the most serious penalties that a state can impose on an individual in terms of the loss of liberty, or the rights to safety and security.

The process of bargaining on behalf of clients in criminal proceedings presents distinct challenges. More generally, Canadian courts have endorsed a perspective on the nature of negotiation that considers it like a kind of card game,[1] as in poker, where misdirection, bluffing, and deception are an accepted part of the play (Woolley *et al.*, 466–477). This common characterization presents discrete complications for legal professionals, who may be more broadly bounded by duties like those described by the integrity rule noted above, as well as numerous other obligations requiring honesty.[2]

While there is no general rule about what is permissible in negotiations for lawyers or others, at least one provincial lawyer regulator has explicitly required that "a lawyer must not lie or mislead another lawyer" and also imposes proactive duties to correct misinformation and possible misapprehensions, subject to overarching duties including things like confidentiality.[3] In terms of either these various legal duties, or of ethical considerations more generally, think about the ethical obligations of the articling student in the following scenario.

NEGOTIATION SCENARIO: Suraida's "Hypothetical" DUI Negotiation[4]

Suraida is an articling student friend of yours, working at a small criminal defence firm in a big city in Canada. She calls you on the phone one day, seeking your ethical expertise in negotiations, based on what she says is a "hypothetical situation." Her "imaginary" client has been charged with impaired driving, though there is no direct evidence of his blood alcohol level. Suraida asks you, "What if the arrest records showed the client had repeatedly said he had nothing to drink, but had admitted privately to us that he had several drinks in the hours before driving?"

Suraida wants to know in this kind of a situation, if she was tasked with negotiating with the Crown to withdraw the charges, what limits are there on the actions she could take. Based on the ethical obligations described above, consider the implications of each of the following options, that Suraida could:

1. Say nothing;
2. Say the client had nothing to drink;
3. Say the client was not impaired; or
4. Say there is no direct evidence the client was impaired.

Continued

Discussion Questions

1. As a preliminary matter, if Suraida is referencing a real-life situation, and not something she has made up as a hypothetical, do you think she breached her ethical and legal obligations to her client by talking to you?[5]

2. Where does Suraida get her authority to disclose any information in a resolution discussion?

3. Is saying nothing to the Crown dishonest in these circumstances, but an appropriate exception in other criminal law cases?

4. Even if taken as an imagined dilemma, can you think of further preparations Suraida would need to make before she talks to the Crown?

5. As discussed later in this chapter, in addition to seeking resolution, one function of bargaining is an exchange of information. In this hypothetical, what information should Suraida be prepared to disclose or to protect in the course of negotiations with the Crown?

THE ETHICAL OBLIGATION OF CIVILITY IN CANADIAN LAW

"Civility" in legal proceedings is an important ethical requirement for legal professionals, which can be enforced by the courts. The idea of civility in Canadian law has at least two parts (Woolley, 178–179). On the one hand, civility relates to a general understanding of appropriate communications between justice system professionals, and includes recognition of the need for politeness and courtesy. This includes obvious examples, like not insulting other people, avoiding the use of profanity, or not employing excessive language in criticism, especially personal or *ad hominem* attacks on others.

Some recent breaches in Canadian law suggest the wide scope of this ethical obligation. For example, a BC lawyer faced professional discipline, in part for not using the title "Mr." in referring to opposing counsel, comparing that lawyer to a "Great Ape" and calling him "stupid or dishonest" in communications (*Harding*).[6] In one of the leading cases that was upheld at the Supreme Court of Canada, a Quebec lawyer was sanctioned for various criticisms in a private note, including accusing a judge of acting like a "coward" (*Doré*).[7] In another BC case, a lawyer was sanctioned, in part, for swearing at a police officer in a courtroom hallway (*Johnson*).[8]

On the other hand, civility also includes a more substantive aspect, which requires lawyers and others to do or refrain from doing things in proceedings if they are detrimental to the administration of justice. For example, procedural tactics that rely on technical requirements or are undertaken with the goal to vex opposing counsel are sometimes referred to as "sharp practice," which is explicitly recognized and prohibited by the professional rules (FLSC, *Model Code*, 7.2-2), and may be also subject to court-imposed sanctions, like the awarding of costs (*Jodoin*).[9]

As both an ethical and legal obligation, the requirement of civility comes from several different sources, but affects all participants in the justice system in Canada. So, for example, while "civility" is not explicitly set out or defined in lawyer codes of conduct, some rules reference the requirement to be "civil" with all persons (FLSC, *Model Code*, 5.1-5, 7.2-1), which has been upheld by the Supreme Court as implicating "civility" more generally (*Groia*). Ontario's legal regulator also oversees the paralegal profession in that province. By contrast to lawyers, the professional rules governing Ontario paralegals do explicitly incorporate an obligation to act with civility (LSO, r 2.01 (3)).

As in the *Jodoin* case, courts may also enforce this obligation. Superior-level trial courts have an inherent discretion in Canadian law to oversee the manner and conduct of proceedings before them, but also exercise broad authority to sanction conduct, and to support legal regulators who may enforce professional sanctions for behaviour both in and outside the courtroom (*Doré*; *Johnson*). In this case, since it is regarded as a general advocacy requirement, courts may independently sanction breaches of civility against lawyers, but also against others, including self-represented litigants (*Radonicich*).[10]

One historical rationale for civility ethics to enjoin legal services professionals is to promote respect for the justice system. However, when viewed through the lens of theories about conflict resolution, what is understood as civility in professional ethics is also a set of practices than can encourage effective conflict management and resolution.

Civility is neither mere politeness nor the absence of conflict; rather, civil behaviour is conduct that is professional and collegial in the midst of a dispute. Legal professionals working in the justice system, like lawyers and others including paralegals, notaries, and social workers, often exist in a tension between fiercely advocating for the interests of their clients, while at the same time problem-solving towards a resolution. This tension can result in confusion and stress when determining what to do in a large array of bargaining situations.

Appropriate conflict resolution and management skills provide tools that enable legal professionals to defend and advance their clients' interests, which includes understanding the purpose and function of acting with civility. Thus, skills and techniques for effective conflict management can both facilitate resolution and also increase the likelihood that those who bargain on behalf of clients in criminal proceedings demonstrate appropriate ethical and professional behaviours. Consider the civility obligation in law in the context of the following case study.

CASE STUDY: A "Rustic Rambo"[11]

In 2009, a client came to Gerry Laarakker's small-town law office in Vernon, British Columbia. The client had a teenaged daughter who, in September of that year, was accused of shoplifting from a local retail store. In November, the client received a "demand letter" from the retailer's external legal counsel in Ontario. The letter requested payment of $521.97 as a "Settlement Amount" for a potential civil claim for theft, damages, and conversion. The letter also noted the possibility of criminal proceedings, and indicated "if this amount is not paid, I may receive specific instructions, whether or not to arrange for a law firm in your jurisdiction to commence legal proceedings."

The practice of retailers sending "demand letters" in response to shoplifting is common, but one that raises serious ethical and legal questions as to its legitimacy in Canadian law. In this instance, Laarakker also knew some personal details about the teenager involved, who suffered from a mental health issue, which was known to be correlated to impulsive behaviour such as shoplifting. In addition to questioning the legal claim in the letter, the lawyer also reported feeling some sympathy for the parent, faced with managing the behaviour of the troubled youth.

Laarakker accepted the case and took steps to find out more about the retailer's actions online. In the course of his investigations, the lawyer came across a blog site that contained postings from other parents who had received similar letters from retailers. Laarakker posted comments to the site saying that the practice gave other "lawyers a bad name," that the letters relied on "intimidation and blackmail," that he "hated those sleazy operators," and that, "speaking as a lawyer," the claims had little chance of success. Laarakker also faxed a letter to the lawyer from Ontario, suggesting their demand to his client was "insulting" and "stupid," that the practice was a "scam," admonishing them to "become a real lawyer," and accusing them of "bullying."

The Ontario lawyer complained to the Law Society of British Columbia. In the disciplinary proceeding that followed, Laarakker admitted he had been rude. However, he justified his uncivil behaviour as an appropriate response to what he regarded as the Ontario's lawyer's own breach of ethics. Laarakker also explained that the situation had provoked a strong personal reaction, because of his sympathy for the parent's struggle in managing their daughter's health.

Case Study Discussion

Consider the ethical obligations in this case study, particularly in relation to questions of "civility." For example, when and how might an assertion about the possibility of future criminal and civil legal liability, as in the demand letter in the case study, be perceived as an unethical threat rather than as a statement of fact?

Continued

In this case study, there are interests that extend beyond the simple question of legal rights. These extra-legal concerns often have a priority for clients and may make some willing to forgo their rights in order to resolve matters quickly. All negotiators should also be aware that these extra-legal interests can exacerbate legal conflicts if left unaddressed. In this instance, the situation was further complicated by Laarakker's apparent emotional investment, which likely prompted some intemperate language, in both public and private communications.

This case study presents an example of where the "objective criteria" that are an important part of interest-based negotiations are contested, in this case involving the legal merit of the claim underlying the dispute. If a factually similar situation was the subject of a resolution discussion, rather than take an adversarial position and to insist on a position in law, are there other options or steps that a bargainer could consider in anticipation?

Does the fact that Laarakker's criticism of demand letters appears to have some substantive merit, along with the relatively mild critical language (e.g., no profanity or extensive hyperbole), excuse or mitigate the nature of the incivility in this case?

Is it the specific language or the circumstances, or some combination of the two, that determines whether communications or behaviour are inappropriate? What if someone used appropriate language, but said it with a consistently sarcastic tone,[12] or alternatively, said something inappropriate, but later excused the behaviour either as inadvertent, or as a failed attempt at humour?[13]

In the end, despite his explanations, Laarakker was found to have breached his professional lawyer obligations. The Law Society disciplinary panel held that, if he had legal and ethical concerns, his proper course was to institute a formal complaint through the legal regulator. Given this, the BC regulator determined that the blog comments and letter were a "marked departure" from acceptable professional standards and fined Laarakker $1,500 and costs.

One last thing to note related to communications, civility, and differ-ent bargaining styles. In some cases, individual bargainers may provoke conflict through uncivil behaviour as a result of their personal adversarial approach, or because of a loss of judgement and temperament in the moment. How can a bargainer anticipate these kinds of behaviours be-forehand to constructively adapt their own style?

While this case study highlights the ethical and legal duty of civility in bargaining, the propriety and effectiveness of professional communi-cations more generally is discussed next, as part of the need to prepare and develop a strategic approach to negotiations.

PRACTICAL SKILLS FOR CONFLICT RESOLUTION: SUGGESTED STRATEGIES

In our view, approaches to bargaining in criminal law can be best under-stood as involving two vital and interlinked phases. Here, negotiation is a process that should be considered from the viewpoints of both prepar-ation and implementation. However, bargaining can be very dynamic, so while we make a distinction, it's best to regard the preparatory and action phases as "two sides of the same coin," in the sense they are often simultaneously complementary and mutually informing. Understanding conflict on a conceptual level can help to frame it and provide a critical path of steps through which it moves towards resolution. More prag-matically, there are actions that bargaining professionals can take in advance and in the negotiation itself to address conflicts effectively as they arise. The following are some suggested strategies.

"Know Yourself": Managing Your Emotional Responses

It is an ancient aphorism that one should "know thyself." An important preparatory step in negotiations is to be self-aware and to "check-in" to honestly reflect about what in any conflict situation may be most upsetting or bothersome. This mindful self-awareness may be espe-cially important in criminal law bargaining, given its inherently public, conflictual, and frequently sensitive nature. Put another way, in criminal resolution discussions it can be useful to "take your emotional temperature" (Fisher and Shapiro) by assessing how you are feeling. It is also important to check the environmental thermometer more generally, prior to and during a bargaining situation, to understand how subjective feelings may have influenced the other side in a negotiation.

Emotional reactions can serve to reveal your own interests, as well as the interests of those representing other parties. But in other situations emotions can present as a barrier to effective conflict resolution and management. This may be particularly the case when the emotions are triggered not by the substance of the matters in dispute, but on the basis of something lateral or peripheral to the conflict.

Emotional triggers can be apparent, but also probably are the result of a range of things like involuntary cognitive biases. In the case study noted above, the lawyer appeared very much aware of his sympathy to extra-legal circumstances. Even when apparent, it's important to remember that emotional factors can affect both the clients and their representatives. But the subconscious is not entirely under our control, and cognitive pitfalls can be an embedded source of dysfunctional emotions as well.

For example, a "halo effect" can occur (Thorndike), where positive or negative prejudices are based on deeply held, sometimes irrational, beliefs or associations. These prejudices could trigger negative perceptions about someone in a negotiation, for example if they reminded another party of someone they disliked. Another common phenomenon in human interaction is the fundamental attributional error. This is an error in thinking where people prejudge by tending to attribute internal motivations to explain the behaviour of others. What this means in criminal law is that many will judgementally assess an accused negatively as having been motivated by an internal moral or character flaw, concluding the person is "bad" and deserving of approbation, while de-emphasizing or ignoring what may be important precipitating contexts (Dripps). In criminal law negotiations, though, such situational factors may in the end be determinative of guilt, can provide legal defences, or could mitigate penalty, so it's important to be aware of how such hidden biases can affect emotions. Ultimately, negotiators in all settings should note the potential for a variety of common cognitive biases to cause emotional reactions, which can alter the course of legal procedures like bargaining (Weinstein).

One issue related to managing personal emotional responses is self-care strategies. These are discussed in more detail in the final chapter. For now, it's enough to note that such approaches can significantly bolster individual capacity to recognize and manage stress quickly when it is experienced, and to address external negotiating stressors while staying alert and calm. In the practical context, this increased focus can help us to manage our own behavioural reactions, but also to accurately "read" and attend to the nuances of both verbal and non-verbal communications (Peters), such as through body language. This includes important indicators of mood such as smiling, open or closed body movements, nodding, eye contact, and sitting forward. One technique in human communications that can be helpful in negotiations is to encourage reciprocal collaboration by "mirroring" positive emotions and constructive behaviours (Blake *et al.*, 203–204).

One of the best ways to manage emotional responses is to emphasize and validate by referencing objective criteria (Roberts and Wright, 1480–82). This includes preparing by doing things like thoroughly interviewing witnesses, consulting appropriate experts, undertaking legal research, examining exhibits or locations, and collecting empirical data, like experience with sentencing ranges. Taking these steps in advance can not only help to facilitate the specific strategy, but also help to implement it on a neutral basis by re-grounding negotiations that might get bogged down in a highly charged or emotional issue.

Communicate Clearly: Ask Questions and Be Curious

As highlighted in Chapter 1, a key element of integrative bargaining is to discover the opposing party's *interests*. Opposing interests can be conceived of as the submerged, larger portion of the iceberg of what is motivating them, below the visible *position* they first articulate or set out. The questioning phase starts before the negotiation, as noted above, with open investigation to prepare as much as possible.

One risk in proceedings is another error in thinking called confirmation bias, which in criminal law can lead to "tunnel vision." This psychological phenomenon has resulted in multiple miscarriages of the criminal justice system over the years (MacFarlane), when individuals make presumptions and engage in results-oriented reasoning, rather than using open inquiry and critical thinking. A closer look at the case of Donald Marshall, one well-known instance of a wrongful conviction based in part on this phenomenon, is included in the next chapter as part of an examination of the distinct roles of defence and Crown counsel in negotiations.

Other psychosocial research related to negotiation, and to bargaining in criminal law, supports generally accepted and taught techniques like active listening and open-ended questioning (Roberts and Wright, 1478). One way to avoid cognitive errors and to discover interests is to prepare direct and clear questions, anticipating contingent follow-ups depending on the nature of the responses. For client interviews, asking direct, open-ended questions like, "what is most important to you in this situation?" or "what most needs to change in order for this situation to be resolved?" or "what would your ideal outcome here be and why?" can be helpful. It might be helpful to ask even more open-ended questions like, "is there anything I should know about that you haven't yet told me?"

Whether with clients or at the bargaining table, balancing open question techniques to encourage elaboration and elicit information with active listening, patience in hearing responses, and even using silence to provoke further commentary are steps that, when combined with specific negotiating techniques, are likely to improve the quality and amount of information gained in the process (Herman, 59, 95–96).

Recognizing Conflict Style: Build on Your Strengths

As noted above, emotional investments and reactions can impede the capacity to manage conflict effectively in negotiations. While planning and strategy can help individuals improve bargaining outcomes, self-awareness about personal negotiating style can also help.

A prepared strategy can be an important touchstone, especially in the spontaneity of bargaining sessions, where one may respond organically without prior planning to unexpected factors.

We are all somewhat predictable and, depending upon the issue that arises, may be more or less naturally inclined to accommodate, compromise, collaborate, or compete based on our personal histories and personalities. Numerous tools are available to help people learn about their personalities generally and conflict styles specifically (Antonioni). Unless we are intentional and mindful, we are more likely to rely upon innate resolution methods based on cognitive errors, like those discussed above, or default approaches, often deeply embedded in our own personal psychological makeup, which may not be the most effective.

For instance, while it can be effective to collaborate with others who are also collaborating or compromising, if we try to collaborate with someone who is intent on domination, we may not end up serving the best interests of clients. In this case, personal awareness that our own preferred or default conflict style may not be effective is paramount, and it provides an opportunity to adapt appropriately to the approach and tactics of our counterpart. This does not imply that it is necessarily prudent to abandon the styles of interaction that seem most natural to us. It simply means it is wise to recognize the approaches and techniques being employed, to take stock of the situation, and to fit our conflict management style to the situation.

Many negotiators in criminal law find practically that bargaining requires shifts in tactics (Roberts and Wright, 1477). That is, even where a collaborative overall approach is adopted, in a single negotiation, some steps in the process may require alternate strategies. For example, the uncertain application of law, in criminal law involving situations that frequently touch on the fundamental rights of individuals, presents issues that are not always possible to address by agreement or collaborative resolution. In this circumstance, it may be necessary to take a position and be prepared to defend it adversarially, within the limits of the professional and ethical considerations considered earlier in this chapter.

Be Flexible: Adapt to the Context

As suggested in the focus on personal style, possible responses to conflict are often framed as being categorized in several types. When faced with conflict, people can choose to compete, compromise, collaborate, avoid, or accommodate the conflict (Johnson and Johnson). A comprehensive collaborative approach focused on interests is usually optimal. However, in some circumstances, preparing to respond utilizing one of these other approaches to conflict may also be appropriate.

Within an interest-based bargaining model, all negotiators should develop short- and long-term "best alternatives to a negotiated agreement" or BATNAs, which account for these potential differences in approach. These "best" alternatives consider the relative risks of a particular position or steps in the negotiating process. Such risk analysis is likely to be especially beneficial in more complex criminal matters, which may involve multiple stages, individuals, or charges. So, for example, an initial BATNA calculation in a matter involving a number of alleged criminal acts would include an assessment of the likelihood of acquittal or conviction on each count. Alternatively, both defence and Crown counsel would want to have some sense of the likely sentence a particular judge (if known)[14] might impose after either a plea to all or some of the charges, or after a conviction at trial (Roberts and Wright, 1479–80).

Canada's justice *system* means that initial consideration of alternatives may shift as proceedings progress or over time. It's sometimes said that "justice delayed is justice denied." On this point, some research suggests that a failure to agree in resolution discussions may in fact open up later opportunities for plea arrangements, in part because of concerns about unfair effects related to delay (NACDL). This research may be especially applicable to less serious criminal offences (Roberts, 1089), where resolution of minor charges might be seen to better prevent injustice and save resources. In Canada, concerns about delay are a broader constitutional imperative, in which the Supreme Court has recently imposed limits which require criminal matters to be resolved on a timely basis (*Jordan*).

Bargainers in criminal proceedings need to account for the fact that BATNA assessments may be contingent on further developments in a case. This includes the passage of time noted above, as well as the possibility of additional circumstances discovered through preparation and investigation for negotiation or subsequently, as to the admissibility of evidence or the applicability of precedent. For example, one obligation of counsel is to not refrain from bringing to the attention of a decision maker a previous case that is binding on the court (FLSC, *Model Code*, 5.1-2 (i)). Sometimes bargainers may disagree about the value of a previous case as objective criteria to assess the one before them.

When there is a basic dispute about the relevance of precedent, negotiators may have to compromise in the short term, by agreeing to disagree as to its applicability. Later, in a competitive mode, advocates can then argue adversarially about it in court, and wait for the judge to determine its relevance. If such a ruling was not dispositive of the case but affected a procedural point, the judge's ruling might require further BATNA adjustments on the ultimate risks for clients in respect of possible outcomes.

Probably the most serious risk assessment in criminal law is considering what would happen in the event of an adverse ruling or verdict. Whatever the ultimate course of action, our system includes respect for rule of law, which requires the acceptance of the authority of the court and its determinations. Of course, even a decision thought to be "bad" or "incorrect" is rightly subject to reasonable and merited criticism about its legal reasoning, and usually also subject to further possible review. What to do and the relative likelihood of success on appeal is also part of the ongoing BATNA calculation. In the end, flexible adaptation to the context, by anticipating alternatives and preparing for a range of outcomes, using a variety of appropriate response styles, is an important approach and strategy in all negotiations.

Collaborate: Resist the Impulse to Dominate; Be Civil

Partly because it is human nature to want to win and partly because we are schooled in an adversarial paradigm, justice system participants often first think about a conflict as a competition where there is a winner and a loser. Thinking about conflict in a competitive way can be unhelpful, since it can promote "all or nothing" behaviour. This kind of competitive mindset is likely one cause of breaches of the overall civility obligation, and can also raise ethical and regulatory issues as discussed above. It is generally best to seek to resolve a conflict through collaboration, seeking to realize the opportunities that are presented by the dispute for creation of new value (Mayer).

Collaboration is more likely to produce a win-win solution. Discovering and empathizing with the other party by imagining the situation from their perspective can help parties to craft solutions to conflicts in which all parties gain something. For example, in plea bargaining, if a conversation becomes heated between counsel, it is a good idea to employ some of the techniques described previously to communicate carefully and clearly, and to try to learn more about the other side's interests, rather than trying to "beat" the other party in an argument. Resisting the impulse to dispute all issues adversarially, and looking for solutions that are "wins" for the other side can pay off in the long term.

One specific strategy to help negotiations stay on track is through framing and anchoring at the outset of bargaining. There is only a little research on the use of these strategies in criminal law proceedings (Roberts and Wright, 1483–85). However, studies show that framing a negotiation by being the first party to make an offer can advantage those who make the attempt. This action is called anchoring, which is a situation in which the first value given to an item has a strong effect on the assessment of its ultimate worth (Tversky and Kahneman, 621–622).

Negotiators who set extreme initial offers to anchor bargaining may frame a negotiation session in their favour. If unreasonable and indefensible, such very low or very high offers might be regarded as illegitimate, or exacerbate competitive instincts, so advance work to reasonably support and defend an anchor, and to maintain a collaborative approach, is crucial. However, where defensible, starting with an optimistic offer may be beneficial, especially for representatives of an accused in criminal matters. There is some evidence, for example, that criminal defence counsel who do not anchor negotiations risk having their dispute framed by the anchoring demands of the prosecution in things like sentencing (Englich *et al.*, 712, 716).

Respond Mindfully and Reflectively

In many cases, the underlying causes of a conflict may be things we cannot change. For example, as criminal justice system practitioners, we work in a system that is hierarchical, complex, stressful, and busy. While we cannot significantly alter the broader institutional and environmental conditions, we can change how we respond to the pressures that the system exerts upon us (Caspersen).

One particular feature of the modern criminal justice system we should pay a little attention to here is the increasing use of indirect communications. As the case study of the "Rustic Rambo" highlighted earlier shows, indirect communications can further complicate an underlying legal dispute. Electronic communication to facilitate bargaining and to negotiate directly is now pervasive via the Internet, in online forums, through emails, and on other platforms. The next chapter also examines the modern challenge of negotiating online in some more detail, as part of the broader challenge of "negotiating across differences." But it's best to remember that bargaining does not start with the open of a formal session, and may be framed, whether online or in person, by a range of initial communications and actions, all of which involve information important to resolution discussions about a dispute.

In either setting, and from the start of interactions with the opposition, each side can be regarded as engaging in a strategic exchange of information (Roberts and Wright, 1487–88). The information revealed at all steps can show interests on both sides of a criminal negotiation, provide a measure of discovery for the defence, give a sense of the respective "theories of the case," demonstrate the strength of evidence, or provide information related to things like sentencing and alternative measures. In the hypothetical scenario presented earlier in this chapter, the articling student presented a situation in which she knew additional information, apparently not available to the Crown. One of Suraida's considerations would be what can and ought to be disclosed. As a broad matter, one thing to consider in planning the approach and in specific bargaining interactions is to determine what information in advance you wish to find out, what information you may choose to reveal—subject to factors like privacy obligations—and what information you may want or be obliged to protect (Herman, 59, 95–96).

So, for example, to protect information that might be subject to confidentiality or solicitor-client privilege, a bargainer could use a number of different tactics to deflect the inquiry. This could include ignoring a question from the opposing side, changing the topic, ruling the question out of bounds, asking a question in response, reframing and asking a different question, and either over- or under-answering (Herman, 78, 84–85). Mindfully and reflectively considering these issues in advance, and then carefully employing these and the other techniques and strategic tips set out in this chapter, increases the likelihood that bargaining, directly or indirectly, in one session or across multiple negotiations, will lead to successful outcomes.

SUMMARY

This chapter has taken a closer look at conflict resolution theory, and its place within bargaining in Canadian criminal law. We have identified the competencies of negotiation, and addressed additional professional issues in criminal negotiations, which were further contextualized in an ethical scenario that dealt with the ethical issues in the disclosure of information. We also examined the ethical obligation of civility in law and communications, and highlighted a recent case in which this issue created challenges for a BC lawyer. We concluded this chapter by examining some practical strategies that can facilitate a successful interest-based negotiation, pointing out some specific techniques and tips, as well as pitfalls, in bargaining. Next, we expand on the approaches and strategies set out in this and in the first chapter, to look at negotiation issues arising in different specific criminal contexts.

SUGGESTIONS FOR FURTHER READING

Advocates' Society. *Principles of Civility for Advocates.* 2009. <https://www. advocates.ca/Upload/Files/PDF/Advocacy/BestPracticesPublications/ Principles_of_Civility_English.pdf>. Accessed February 3, 2019.

Antonioni, D. "Relationship Between the Big Five Personality Factors and Conflict Management Styles." (1998) 9:4 *Int J Confl Manag* 336–355.

Findley, Keith A., and Michael S. Scott. "The Multiple Dimensions of Tunnel Vision in Criminal Cases." (2006) *Wis L Rev* 291.

Forsyth, Donelson R. *Group Dynamics*, 5th ed. Boston: Wadsworth Cengage Learning, 2009.

Mayer, B. *The Dynamics of Conflict Resolution: A Practitioner's Guide*. San Francisco: Jossey-Bass, 2000.

Messina, Toni. "Innocent People Who Plead Guilty." *Above the Law*, 2018, July 23. <https://abovethelaw.com/2018/07/innocent-people-who-plead-guilty/>. Accessed February 5, 2019.

Sorensen, Jane. "Courthouse Hallway Comments Can Cost Lawyers in Penalties." *Canadian Lawyer*, 2018, April 4. <https://www.canadianlawyermag.com/legalfeeds/courthouse-hallway-comments-can-cost-lawyers-in-penalties-15546/>. Accessed February 3, 2019.

Spratt, Michael. "Why Plea Bargains Can Be a Deal with the Devil." *Canadian Lawyer*, 2017, January 16.

Thompson, L., M. Neale, and M. Sinaceur. "The Evolution of Cognition and Biases in Negotiation Research: An Examination of Cognition, Social Perception, Motivation, and Emotion," in M.J. Gelfand and J.M. Brett, editors, *The Handbook of Negotiation and Culture*. Stanford, CA: Stanford Business Books, 2004, 7–44.

ENDNOTES

1. *Westcom TV Group Ltd v CanWest Global Broadcasting Inc*, [1996] BCJ No 1638, 26 BCLR (3d) 311, at para 18 (BCSC).

2. See for example, FLSC, *Model Code* at 3.2-7m that requires a lawyer to never: (a) knowingly assist or encourage any dishonesty, fraud, crime, or illegal conduct; and (b) do or omit to do anything that the lawyer ought to know assists in or encourages any dishonesty, fraud, crime, or illegal conduct by a client or others; and (c) instruct a client or others on how to violate the law and avoid punishment.

3. Law Society of Alberta, *Code of Conduct*, 7.2-2 and 7.2-5, respectively.

4. Adapted from Woolley *et al.*, editors, "Scenario Five," at 476.

5. Probably. Under the FLSC *Model Code*, a lawyer may disclose confidential information in some circumstances, for example, to another lawyer to seek legal or ethical advice about proposed conduct (3.3-6), or with client consent (3.3-2 [1]), but must generally hold all information concerning the business and affairs of the client in strict confidence. If Suraida's scenario is based on real circumstances, she may also have breached solicitor-client privilege, recognized by the Supreme Court of Canada as both a right and a fundamental principle of justice; see *Lavallee*.

6. *Harding*, at paras 89, 92, and 94 respectively.

7. *Doré* at para 10, where the lawyer also described the judge as "petty," "pedantic," "aggressive," "unjust," and "loathsome."

8. *Johnson* at paras 1 and 21; the lawyer took a police officer's refusal of a request to be aggressive, his profanity appeared intemperate, and the two also faced off in a close physical confrontation.

9. *Jodoin*, where the Supreme Court upheld an award of costs against a criminal defence counsel for repeated attempts to have judges removed from hearings as a "deliberate abuse of the justice system," at para 3.

10. Which applied the civility guidelines of a private lawyers' professional organization to a self-represented litigant; see Advocates' Society, *Principles of Civility for Advocates*.

11. Details and background summarized from Rankin, "Rustic Rambo." See also *Laarakker (Re)*, 2011, LSBC 29 CanLII.

12. *Groia*, where one of the criticisms of the appellant was that he consistently used an inappropriate tone to, *inter alia*, identify opposing counsel for the *Ontario Securities Commission* as "government lawyers."

13. In disciplinary matters involving civility for lawyers, intent may not matter. See *Foo v LSBC*, where a BC lawyer was disciplined for making a threat in saying "I should shoot you" to a social worker, which he unsuccessfully defended as an ill-advised attempt at a joke to criticize the child apprehension policies of the social services agency.

14. There is very little evaluative evidence of individual judge performance in Canada; however, in our anecdotal experience, the reputation of a judge based on personal characteristics and temperament, as well as past decisions, may often be considered an important factor in the outcome of proceedings.

REFERENCES

Advocates' Society. *Principles of Civility for Advocates.* 2009. <https://www.
advocates.ca/Upload/Files/PDF/Advocacy/BestPracticesPublications/
Principles_of_Civility_English.pdf>. Accessed February 3, 2019.

Antonioni, D. "Relationship Between the Big Five Personality Factors and
Conflict Management Styles." (1998) 9:4 *Int J Confl Manag* 336–355.

Barreau du Quebec v Doré, [2012] 1 SCR 395, 2012 SCC 12 [*Doré*].

Bercovitch, Jacob, Victor Kremenyuk, and I. William Zartman, editors. *The
Sage Handbook of Conflict Resolution.* Thousand Oaks, CA: Sage, 2009.

Blake, Susan Heath, Julie Browne, and Stuart Sime. *A Practical Approach to
Dispute Resolution.* Oxford: Oxford University Press, 2016.

Bolton, Lisa, and Gerald Griffiths. "Workplace Harassment: Understanding
an Employer's Risks and Obligations." *Canadian HR Reporter*, 2018,
September 1.

Bourdeau, Valerie. *Intimidation of Justice System Participants: General
Overview of Literature and Report.* Ottawa: Publications Canada, 2012.
<http://publications.gc.ca/collections/collection_2018/jus/J4-57-2012-
eng.pdf>. Accessed February 1, 2019.

Brown, Karen. *An Exploratory Analysis of Violence and Threats Against Lawyers.*
MA Thesis, Simon Fraser University, Department of Criminology, 2012.

Caspersen, D. *Changing the Conversation: The 17 Principles of Conflict
Resolution.* New York: Penguin Books, 2015.

Criminal Code of Canada RSC 1985, c, C-46 [*Criminal Code*].

Dripps, Donald A. "Fundamental Retribution Error: Criminal Justice and
the Social Psychology of Blame." (2003) 56 *Van L Rev* 1383.

Englich, Burt, Thomas Mussweiler, and Fritz Strack. "The Last Word in
Court—The Hidden Disadvantage for the Defence." (2005) 29 *Law &
Hum Behav* 705.

Federation of Law Societies. *Model Code of Professional Conduct* [FLSC,
Model Code], as amended March 14, 2017. <https://flsc.ca/wp-content/
uploads/2018/03/Model-Code-as-amended-March-2017-Final.pdf>.
Accessed January 20, 2019.

Felstiner, W., and A. Sarat. "The Emergence and Transformation of Disputes:
Naming, Blaming and Claiming ..." (1980) 15 *Law & Soc'y Rev* 631.

Fisher, Roger, and Daniel Shapiro. *Beyond Reason: Using Emotions as You Negotiate*. New York: Viking Penguin, 2005.

Foo v Law Society of British Columbia, 2017 BCCA 151 CanLII [*Foo v LSBC*].

Furlong, G. *The Conflict Resolution Toolbox*. Mississauga, ON: John Wiley & Sons, 2005.

Gadlin, H., I. Macduff, and A. K. Schneider. "Of Babies and Bathwater: Innovation and Continuity in Negotiation Pedagogy," in Christopher Honeyman, James R. Coben, and Andrew Wei-Min Lee, editors, *Educating Negotiators for a Connected World*. Saint Paul, MN: DRI Press, 2013.

Groia v Law Society of Upper Canada, 2018 SCC 27 CanLII [*Groia*].

Harding (Re), 2013 LS BC 25 CanLII [*Harding*].

Herman, Nicholas G. *Plea Bargaining*, 3rd ed. Huntington, NY: Juris Publishing, 2012.

Johnson (Re), 2016 LSBC 20 CanLII [*Johnson*].

Johnson, D. W., and F. P. Johnson. *Joining Together: Group Theory and Group Skills*. Essex, UK: Pearson Education, 1994.

Laarakker (Re), 2011, LSBC 29 CanLII.

Lavallee, Rackel & Heintz v Canada, 2002 3 SCR 209 [*Lavallee*].

Law Society of Alberta. *Code of Conduct*. April 26, 2018. <https://dvbat5idxh7ib.cloudfront.net/wp-content/uploads/2017/01/14211909/Code.pdf>. Accessed March 1, 2019.

Law Society of Ontario (LSO). *Paralegals Rules of Conduct*. <https://lso.ca/about-lso/legislation-rules/paralegal-rules-of-conduct/rule-2>. Accessed April 7, 2019.

Leering, Michele. "Conceptualizing Reflective Practice for Legal Professionals." (2014) 23 *Journal of Law and Social Policy* 83–106.

MacFarlane, Bruce. "Wrongful Convictions: The Effect of Tunnel Vision and Predisposing Circumstances in the Criminal Justice System." <http://www.attorneygeneral.jus.gov.on.ca/inquiries/goudge/policy_research/index.html>. Accessed February 8, 2019.

Macfarlane, Julie. *The New Lawyer: How Settlement Is Transforming the Practice of Law*. Vancouver: UBC Press, 2008.

Mayer, B. *The Dynamics of Conflict Resolution: A Practitioner's Guide*. San Francisco: Jossey-Bass, 2000.

National Association of Criminal Defense Attorneys (NACDL). *The Trial Penalty: The Sixth Amendment Right to Trial on the Verge of Extinction and How to Save It*. Washington, DC: NACDL, 2018. <www.nacdl.org/trialpenaltyreport>.

Peters, Pamela. "Gaining Compliance through Non-Verbal Communication." (2006) 7:1 *Pepp Disp Resol LJ*.

Porter-O'Grady, T. "Embracing Conflict: Building a Healthy Community." (2004) 29 *Health Care Management Review* 181–187.

Putnam, Linda L., and Samantha Rae Powers. "Developing Negotiating Competencies," in Angret F. Hannawa and Brian Spitzberg, editors, *Communication Competencies*. Berlin: De Gruyter Mouton, 2015.

Quebec (Director of Criminal and Penal Prosecutions) v Jodoin, 2017 SCC 26, [2017] 1 SCR 478.

Radonicich v Reamey, 2008 OJ No 2210 (SCJ) [*Radonicich*].

Rankin, Micah. "From Rustic Rambo to Rebel with a Cause," in A. Dodek and A. Woolley, editors, *In Search of the Ethical Lawyer*. Vancouver: UBC Press, 2016, 225–243.

Roberts, Jenny. "Crashing the Misdemeanour System." (2013) 70 *Wash & Lee L Rev* 1089.

Roberts, Jenny, and Ronald F. Wright. "Training for Bargaining." (2016) 57 *Wm & Mary L Rev* 1445.

R v Jordan, 2016 SCC 27 CanLII [*Jordan*].

Thorndike, E. L. "A Constant Error in Psychological Ratings." (1920) 6 *Journal of Applied Psychology* 119.

Tversky, Amos, and Daniel Kahneman. "Anchoring, Information, Expertise, and Negotiation: Insights from Meta-Analysis." (2006) 21 *Ohio St J Disp Resol* 597.

Weinstein, Ian. "Don't Believe Everything You Think: Cognitive Bias in Legal Decision Making." (2003) 8 *Clinical L Rev* 783.

Westcom TV Group Ltd v CanWest Global Broadcasting Inc, [1996] BCJ No 1638, 26 BCLR (3d) 311, at para 18 (BCSC).

Woolley, A. "Integrity in Zealousness: Comparing the Standard Conceptions of the Canadian and American Lawyer." (1996) 9 *Can J L & Juris* 6.

Woolley, A., Richard F. Devlin, Brent Cotter, and John M. Law. *Lawyers' Ethics and Professional Regulation*, 3rd ed. Toronto: LexisNexis, 2017.

CHAPTER 3

Negotiating across Differences: Roles, Social Context, Culture, and Process

LEARNING OBJECTIVES

After reading this chapter, students should have new insight into:

- Role differences of the defence and prosecution in criminal law
- The effects of social context, cultural competence, and professionalism
- Technical competency and procedural differences in negotiating online
- Techniques for building rapport and enhancing communication strategies to effectively negotiate across differences

OVERVIEW

This chapter explores challenges in negotiating across situational and individual differences. It builds on the general discussion of theories and integrative styles using an interest-based approach, as well as the strategies and tactics for effective negotiation presented previously. It considers resolution discussions in criminal law through an examination of differences arising from individual roles and social and procedural variability, and seeks to engage more deeply with a few of the thornier issues complicating criminal law bargaining. In this respect, bargaining is a social interaction among individuals, but it cannot be fully understood without reference to the context in which it takes place.

There is a world of differences that can affect negotiations, based on individual, structural, and procedural circumstances. Our examination starts with a look at the distinguishable role requirements of the Crown and defence counsel. All negotiators have prescribed functions within criminal proceedings, based on their association with either the prosecution or the defence. Negotiation context thus includes an inherent adversarialism within the structure of criminal justice, which creates certain obligations not present in other kinds of bargaining that instead frequently emphasize economic and monetary compensation.

The examination of adversarial roles is illustrated by the presentation of a notorious proceeding in Canadian legal history involving the wrongful conviction of Donald Marshall, a young Nova Scotian of Mi'kmaq ancestry. This case study underscores the importance of role differences, but also serves as a departure point for discussion about cultural factors, including indigeneity, and the need for all negotiators to develop wider cultural competence. Next, as part of our look at procedural context we consider differences in modern negotiations occasioned by the rise of online negotiations, and the emerging need for bargainers to also demonstrate technical competence. We conclude by discussing practical communications techniques and how to build rapport to help identify and overcome these role, culture, and procedural differences. Readers interested in exploring in additional detail the wide range of differences that can affect negotiations, like gender, race, and class, can find suggestions for further reading at the end of this chapter. We highlight these differences in Chapter 6 as part of the discussion of dealing with "difficult" people and discrimination.

ROLES OF DEFENCE AND CROWN COUNSEL

In Chapter 2, we considered some regulatory obligations of legal professionals who negotiate in criminal law. In fact, there is no explicit rule about the ethical limits imposed on bargainers.[1] However, there are some specific professional duties for legal professionals like lawyers that do address plea arrangements in criminal proceedings. While those working in criminal law may be performing different functions, advocating as social workers, acting as paralegals or other legal professionals, or assisting a self-represented person, it's important that everyone has a sense of the general ethical boundaries that guide the participants in criminal law bargaining.

In terms of plea agreements specifically, this includes a lawyer professional rule that authorizes the practice (FLSC, *Model Code*, 5.1-7). Another regulatory obligation sets certain limits on what defence counsel can do in resolution discussions, as follows:

> **5.1-8** A lawyer for an accused or potential accused may enter into an agreement with the prosecutor about a guilty plea if, following investigation,
>
> (a)   the lawyer advises his or her client about the prospects for an acquittal or finding of guilt;
>
> (b)   the lawyer advises the client of the implications and possible consequences of a guilty plea and particularly of the sentencing authority and discretion of the court, including the fact that the court is not bound by any agreement about a guilty plea;
>
> (c)   the client voluntarily is prepared to admit the necessary factual and mental elements of the offence charged; and
>
> (d)   the client voluntarily instructs the lawyer to enter into an agreement as to a guilty plea.

Criminal plea discussions can be a prickly subject, in part because of the growing recognition that people accused of committing crimes may choose to plead guilty for a range of reasons. It might seem counterintuitive that someone would falsely admit to committing a crime. However, research has shown that there are a wide variety of things that can cause someone to confess and enter a plea for something they have not done. This includes a desire to avoid a "penalty" of more severe sentencing if found guilty after a trial (NACDL). It can also include a decision to plead based on interests beyond legal considerations (Sherrin). An interesting contrast to the Canadian experience is that England and the United States permit lawyers to participate in pleading guilty, even though the client might privately maintain their innocence (Sherrin).

However, as reflected in rule 5.1-8 (c) set out above, Canadian courts have determined that a client who accepts a plea bargain must be prepared to voluntarily admit in open court the necessary factual and mental elements of the offences charged (*R v SK*). The professional rules touching on this obligation in plea bargaining appear to place responsibility on the defence to ensure that "false" guilty pleas are not submitted. However, the Supreme Court of Canada has recently confirmed that Crown counsel are also obliged not to proceed with criminal resolution agreements where they know or are concerned, based on evidence, that an accused may be factually innocent (*R v Anthony-Cook*, para 44). On all sides, a court will look to ensure that guilty pleas are voluntary, informed, and unequivocal (*McIlvride-Lister*, para 37).

As attorneys charged with public responsibility to enforce laws on behalf of the state, Crown counsel must consider wider interests in criminal proceedings (Dodek). In Canada, prosecuting lawyers have historically been recognized as having duties to consider the public interest in the effectiveness of the justice system as "mini" ministers of justice (*Boucher*). Lawyer rules and policy guidelines directing Crown Attorneys reflect this traditional role and provide examples of how this affects their approach to criminal resolution discussions. For example, the FLSC *Model Code* notes that "when engaged as a prosecutor, the lawyer's primary duty is not to seek to convict but to see justice is done through a fair trial on the merits. The prosecutor exercises a public function involving much discretion and power and must act fair and dispassionately" (5.1-3 [1]).

The public scope of the prosecutor's obligations means that they have a range of interests to consider, beyond those of their client (the Crown), or those of the opposing party. Typically, Crowns must also consider the views of those involved in a criminal matter, including the victim, the community, and, where applicable, the interests of the investigating agency (PPSC, *Deskbook*, 2.1). In cases where a self- or unrepresented person enters into a resolution discussion, Crown Attorneys must also take special measures to ensure the rights of the accused are protected. This includes advising them of their right to counsel, seeking the assistance of duty counsel in appropriate circumstances, and advising the presiding judicial official. If needed, prosecutors can recommend that adjudicators hold a comprehension hearing in the event of a plea or sentence agreement (PPSC, *Deskbook*, 4.1), so that the court can confirm that the accused appreciates what a "guilty" plea means.

The Public Prosecution Service of Canada's *Deskbook* details the various kinds of resolution discussions that Crown Attorneys may undertake. For example, on charge discussions, this can include agreeing to stay certain counts and to proceed on others or relying on the material facts that support the stayed counts as aggravating factors for sentencing purposes (*Criminal Code*, 725). This policy guideline also highlights the broader role of the Crown as public officials, by setting out unacceptable practices, which include proceeding with unnecessary additional charges to secure a negotiated plea (PPSC, *Deskbook*, 4.2). Other unacceptable practices include a promise in advance not to appeal the sentence imposed at trial (PPSC, *Deskbook*, 4.4.1), or entering into agreements about the facts of the offence that either misleads or appears to mislead the court (PPSC, *Deskbook*, 4.5).

Resolution discussions and plea bargains can play an important role to make the criminal courts work better. However, the commentary to lawyer professional rules governing agreements on a guilty plea also notes that "the public interest in the administration of justice should not be sacrificed in the interest of expediency" (FLSC, *Model Code*, 5.1-8 [1]). Ultimately, the rules, commentary, and other ethical guidelines remind us that efficiency, through the prudent use of bargaining and negotiation in criminal proceedings, must not displace the ultimate fairness of the Canadian justice system.

Consider the ethical and professional obligations of the Crown and defence counsel in the context of the following case study, describing a notorious example of wrongful conviction in Canadian law.

CASE STUDY: Donald Marshall

At age 17, Donald Marshall was sentenced to life in prison for murder in Nova Scotia. Marshall was an Indigenous youth from the Mi'kmaq First Nations community. He was convicted in the death of another 17-year-old, Sandy Seale, an African-Canadian who died on May 28, 1971. In an unusually rapid legal process, Marshall was arrested five days after Seale's death, and convicted after a three-day trial, which occurred less than six months after his initial police detention. On appeal, Marshall's conviction was overturned by the Nova Scotia Court of Appeal. Later, a man named Roy Ebsary was convicted of manslaughter in relation to Seale's death.

It was not until 1990, however, that Donald Marshall was fully exonerated in relation to Seale's death (*Marshall Inquiry*). Donald Marshall's case took place many years ago, as did the inquiry into his wrongful conviction, but similar stereotyping and unconscious biases, a key factor in the case that led to a miscarriage of justice, are still resulting in unjust treatment for marginalized accused persons across Canada. Consider as you read the remainder of this chapter, how, in your negotiations as a legal professional working in the criminal law context, you might work to avoid the factors that produced Donald Marshall's wrongful conviction.

Case Study Discussion

The case of Donald Marshall highlights the role of the prosecution, and the need for the Crown to act in the broader public interest. While the Crown plays a recognized adversarial role, the traditional view is that they "win" by seeing justice done, whether or not they prevail in any given proceeding (FLSC, *Model Code*, 5.1-3 [1]). In the *Marshall* case, the Crown failed to follow some basic steps not only pertinent to negotiation competencies, but also part of their broader professional obligations. Here, this included failing to interview witnesses and to disclose some contradictory evidence to the defence counsel. For its part, defence counsel conducted no independent investigation, and, though aware of prior witness statements, failed to request their disclosure (*Marshall Inquiry*).

In the previous chapter, we noted how unconscious biases can result in errors in thinking. The *Marshall* case presents an example of where, in developing their "theory of the case," police investigators and prosecutors engaged in results-oriented thinking, or "tunnel vision," which led them to emphasize evidence that confirmed their pre-existing presumption that their suspect was culpable. The later Inquiry also highlighted the significant impact of "demeanour evidence." Such evidence is an example of another cognitive mistake called the fundamental attributional error, where people are inclined to assign internal motivations or explanations for behaviour, while diminishing the importance of external factors (Dripps).

In this instance, Marshall's soft speech in court, his bowed head, and his lack of eye contact (*Marshall Inquiry*) were taken as an outward behavioural sign of his internal sense of guilt. It is now generally appreciated that demeanour, including appearance, tone, mannerisms, and attitude, may be affected by different backgrounds and cultural experiences. Eye contact may suggest forthrightness in one context, but might be considered rude in another. While some societies might expect demonstrations of remorse on the admission of guilt, others might expect that judgements be accepted stoically without emotion (Advocates' Society, 57). While questions about demeanour apply to Indigenous participants in the justice system like Donald Marshall, in recent years, courts have expanded their recognition of the importance of differences in other cultural contexts,[2] and of the broad effects of systemic discrimination in the criminal justice system.

In Canada, continuing issues with systemic discrimination involving members of Indigenous communities have led to distinct procedures to address some aspects of criminal allegations in their cultural context. For example, Canada's *Criminal Code* now contains a provision that mandates consideration of individual contexts "with particular attention to the circumstances of Aboriginal offenders" (*Criminal Code*, 718.2 (e)). In such cases, Indigenous accused are entitled to have pre-sentencing or pre-bail disposition *Gladue* reports,[3] which consider cultural and

Continued

individual circumstances as factors in seeking alternatives to detention. The Supreme Court recently noted that, in applying this section, courts "must" take notice of "the history of colonialism, displacement and residential schools" as well as education, economic situation, employment, addictions, mental health, and historically high levels of incarceration of Indigenous peoples (*Ipeelee*).

There continues to be widespread acknowledgement of systemic challenges and racism within Canada's criminal justice system (Ghittens and Cole). Discriminatory treatment of some racial groups within the criminal justice system has been noted by some,[4] and all too often involves controversial practices in law enforcement like "carding," or asking people for ID without reason to suspect an offence, which may unfairly target certain racial and socio-economic groups who face yet further challenges in the legal system like problematic sentencing decisions, and differential experiences in corrections (Tanovich). In terms of Canada's First Nations, Canada's Truth and Reconciliation Commission of Canada (TRC), organized by the parties of the Indian Residential Schools Settlement Agreement, released a report in 2015 that called for recognition of discrimination against Indigenous people in the legal system.

NEGOTIATION SCENARIO: Suraida and Bob—*Gladue* Reports

Suraida is an articling student who represents her client Bob, who has been charged with drunk and disorderly public conduct. Police reports suggest he was stopped after staggering down the street and his speech was slurred, though he initially insisted he had only one beer with a friend. In investigating the matter, Suraida has talked to the friend, who instead says that Bob had several drinks on the night in question. Suraida has also confirmed that Bob is a member of a First Nations community in Northern Ontario, where he was previously convicted for disorderly conducted and for driving while impaired.

Bob has told Suraida that he is seriously distressed by his legal troubles and wants to plead "guilty" to the charge to resolve the matter, as long as he doesn't have to go to jail and risk losing his landscaping job, or be unable to care for his sick father. In resolution discussions with the Crown, Suraida has requested that a pre-disposition report, or a *Gladue* report, be prepared, in accordance with the requirements of the *Criminal Code*, s 718 (2) (e).

Discussion Question

1.   If you were asked to investigate in order to contribute to the anticipated *Gladue* report in this scenario, what are some of the circumstances related to Bob's situation that might be highlighted or further explored and included for the consideration of the court?[5]

CULTURAL CONTEXT IN NEGOTIATIONS

Negotiating across differences includes an appreciation of social and cultural context. Culture can be understood as a way of life, which includes systems of shared meanings and values, often communicated in art and learning, but also in institutional and ordinary behaviour (Hall). From the perspective of legal studies scholars, criminal proceedings often involve these cultural and social contexts, and in many ways, we recreate the social world in legal interactions (Mezey). This includes both formal trials or informal proceedings that are often less transparent (Luban), like resolution discussions and negotiations.

Critical legal studies researchers have had much to say in recent years about problems with how culture and social context intersect the law. For example, in social context, one prominent issue that has received attention is the apparent inability of the criminal justice system to respond effectively to women's allegations of sexual assault. Media reports portray a dismayingly high percentage of assault allegations against women that are regularly dismissed by police as "unfounded" (Doolittle), and also of the small percentage of such cases that actually make it to court.[6] Some have questioned the role of other actors in the court system who may be contributing to the problem, such as defence counsel (Craig), or the judiciary.[7]

It's important to keep in mind that while the legal system operates on the premise that "everyone is equal in the eyes of the law," whether on the basis of gender or culture or other factors more generally, the effects of the criminal justice system are experienced very unevenly by different groups. For instance, certain demographic populations are more likely to be subjected to criminal sanctions than others. This includes those of lower socio-economic status, youth, and racialized people and Indigenous groups, who are far more frequently charged, tried, convicted, and then incarcerated in Canada (Statistics Canada).

Simple differences in social context and culture alone do not wholly account for this phenomenon. In recent years, there has been widespread acknowledgement of systemic challenges and racism within Canada's criminal justice system (Ghittens and Cole). Recall, for example, in the *Marshall* case a lack of cultural competence regarding the accused's testimonial demeanour was a factor in his wrongful conviction. In the time since the *Marshall* case, there has been a growing appreciation of the scope of systemic discrimination on First Nations populations, who are disproportionally sent to jail and currently represent a quarter of Canada's overall prison population (Malakieh).

Increasingly, social context, culture, and respect for diversity are recognized as important dimensions of professional competence. Some have questioned whether legal professional bodies have, in the past, had a sufficiently inclusive concept of competence (Woolley *et al.*, 188–189). In response, many law societies have adopted policies and imposed professional obligations intended to reduce discrimination on racial and other grounds, including gender. Ontario's Law Society now requires its licensees to take steps designed to reduce systemic discrimination in the provision of legal services, including mandatory education (LSO, *Equity, Diversity and Inclusion*), and to express commitment through a "Statement of Principles," to acknowledge an obligation to promote equality, diversity, and inclusion in their professional work (LSO, *Statement of Principles*).

THE SKILLS AND HABITS OF CULTURAL COMPETENCE

A crucial skill needed for legal services professionals is **cultural competence** (Voyvodic). Cultural competence is in some ways analogous to language interpretation. It is an ability to interact and communicate effectively to understand people across cultural differences. An important part of this process is to situate ourselves within a broader perspective. For example, it is useful to reflect on and acknowledge one's own traditions, perhaps even starting with something as simple as considering the holiday periods that are recognized and celebrated. It is important to realize that whatever might be the "norm" within our own experience, we all live and work within a much broader cultural context, in which many different traditions are prevalent. In this respect, it is helpful to cultivate positive attitudes about differences, and to be curious about alternate cultural practices and worldviews.

We grow our cultural competence when we shape our actions around an intention to build understandings between people. This means we need to start from a place of humility, to be respectful and open to different perspectives. It does not mean we have to abandon our own viewpoints, but we should recognize that there are differences in practices, ideas, and opinions, sometimes even within the same cultural group. One way to develop an appreciation of culture and to enhance competence is to maintain and seek to build relations between diverse communities. To build respectful relationships, legal services providers should mindfully seek to avoid using their own personal experience and identity related to things like race, gender, ethnicity, ability, or sexual orientation as the standard by which to assess appropriate behaviour on the part of others.

We've previously identified and discussed mistakes in cognition important in criminal law, and in the bargaining process, like confirmation bias and the fundamental attributional error. One further bias, related to cultural competence, is **implicit bias** (Jolls and Sunstein). Decision-making is often affected by implicit bias, even when people are not being deliberately discriminatory. It's probably commonplace and natural for humans to notice patterns, and to make generalizations. However, if we over-generalize without enough attention to context, we can be incorrect in our assumptions, which can lead to prejudice and a reliance on stereotypes. The human tendency for thoughts that link people in patterns based on generalizations is what psychologists call implicit bias.

Explicit Hollywood-like portrayals of overt, intentional racial discrimination are often knowingly employed and exploited in popular media to make money. Explicit discrimination sometimes occurs in professional settings as well. However, when people are acting in their professional capacities to provide legal services in the criminal justice system, often more common are forms of racial and gender discrimination attributable to unintentional, systemic discrimination and implicit bias. Implicit bias can lead to certain conclusions without our fully being aware of why (Casey). For example, in the context of negotiation, we may drive a "harder bargain" and be less flexible with people we don't relate to well, or trust. If we subconsciously harbour dysfunctional or negative views of certain groups based on erroneous assumptions, or are ignorant of systemic challenges, then individual members of those groups may suffer from relatively adverse treatment in the criminal justice system.

Implicit bias is not always about *negative* stereotypes. Indeed, biased decision-making is often not attributable to a negative response to someone who is "other" but rather a positive response to those we identify with, and therefore more easily empathize with as well. It may not be that we treat people who are different from us badly but rather that we tend more often to treat those who we identify with well. This is called "in-group favouritism" (Galinsky and Moskowitz).

Unfortunately, in the high-paced and stressful environment of criminal practice, we face a work environment rife with risk factors that, as identified below, can make us more likely to rely on implicit bias in decision-making. The following are some strategies, tips, and techniques for how to avoid falling into stereotypical reasoning and making decisions based on implicit bias.

1. Self-Care. If we take care of ourselves, we are better positioned to act reasonably and use better judgement. One of the first and best steps to exercising self-care is to ensure better physical and mental health through enough rest (Casey). In recent years, there has been an increased focus on the stresses experienced by a range of participants in the justice system by workload and other factors, which we consider more fully in the final chapter. However, when negotiating across difference, it is important that bargainers find ways to keep conscious focus on their work, to exercise control over professional environments (Seligman *et al.*, 58), and to manage workloads effectively. It is crucial that we allow ourselves enough time to place decisions and actions in perspective, to not get caught in the dynamics of the moment, or to act unreflectively based on emotion or cognitive errors in bargaining (Jolls and Sunstein).[8]

2. Education. People can decrease their reliance on bias through deliberative cognitive processes (Jolls and Sunstein, 975), including education and training to increase awareness. An attitude that acknowledges the potential effects of bias and stereotyping, together with knowledge and increased skills, are methods to address cultural competence (Voyvodic, 582). The bad news is that while it's better to be conscious of biases, simple awareness by itself may not be sufficient for bargainers to overcome them. The good news is that specific training can likely help (Roberts and Wright, 1484). Consider attending a training session on implicit bias and also explore the references and further reading at the end of this chapter.

3. Openness. It's a good "habit" of cultural competence to take note of the differences between the participants in a resolution discussion (Bryant). It is easier to counter stereotypes that are based in difference if we consciously look right at them and acknowledge them out loud. In some instances, we have found that it can be useful to expressly acknowledge group differences and to share information about our own experiences to develop a culturally competent attitude that reduces the negative effects of assumptions and stereotypes (Voyvodic, 582). Acknowledging differences in a respectful way, rather than ignoring or avoiding mentioning them, can facilitate interactions and help to build communicative rapport.

4. Mitigate Bias with Concrete Action. Develop a strategy that is specific, clear, and concrete, and that also accounts for potentially different cultural understandings (Bryant). The key is to support yourself in contemplating and providing a rationale for decisions that rests on objective criteria (Oliver and Batra, 68–78). It's important to reflectively seek to improve interactions in negotiations, including considering additional reasons for "puzzling" participant behaviour (Bryant). In the moment, do not simply "go with your gut." Anticipate in advance by articulating a basis for your actions and decisions. For example, you could engage in mental "perspective-taking" exercises, in which you imagine yourself in the other person's shoes (Galinsky and Moskowitz).

5. Take Detailed Notes. There is some evidence that taking notes can reduce bias in legal decision-making (Hartley). While note-taking needs to be balanced with listening and comprehension, detailed notes about an ongoing situation can also help improve judgement (Strub and McKimmie). Notes can also serve to refresh memory, and as one more objective metric by which to later assess interactions.

6. Receive and Seek Constructive Criticism. Generally, the people who work with us have a good sense of our strengths and challenges. It can be useful to seek input and feedback from trusted colleagues regarding our past performance. Another form of feedback can be self-initiated and based in quantitative measures. We can keep our own private running lists of statistical outcomes in cases we work on. It can be useful to take a look at the metrics of the results of our own decision-making and cross-reference how our decision-making measures up against problems with over-representation of certain populations in criminal courts and corrections custody.

7. Change Your Experiences with "Others." If we have preconceived notions about certain groups, these can often be changed when we gain new experiences. We can actively seek out ways to increase our contact with members of groups other than our own race, gender, age, religion, or sexual orientation in order to develop comfortability with them. We can learn about, and then work to imagine, "counter-stereotypical" individuals from groups other than our own. It can also be useful to read about positive role models from a marginalized group, especially focussing on role models who counter negative stereotypes about a group (Blair *et al.*).

It can be challenging for everyone to negotiate across difference. To sum up though, scholars who write about cultural competence suggest employing the techniques set out above in the context of several general skills. Here is an example of a framework for organized preparation for intercultural negotiation (Deardorff):

- Cultivate **empathy** for your counterpart through developing a clear understanding of their interests;
- Ensure you both show and consciously seek to **respect** their worldview and traditional practices;
- Work to be **flexible** and willing to adapt behaviours to suit their needs (doing things like, as a woman, wearing a head covering in a meeting at a religious place of worship);
- Be mindfully **curious** about another culture's traditional knowledge;
- Adopt a **growth mindset** to avoid taking on stereotypical assumptions and avoid being defensive. Accept that we are all on a journey of learning more about one another; and
- **Accept ambiguity** as to how people should act politely in the context of social niceties.

These can all be helpful ways to prevent cultural difference from being a barrier to effective negotiation.

TECHNICAL COMPETENCE AND ONLINE NEGOTIATION

Increasingly, communications happen online, through platforms such as email, and by text, Skype, and other social media. The case study of Gerry Laarakker presented in Chapter 2 involved a lawyer who breached his professional civility obligations, after using inappropriate language in a faxed letter and in an online forum. That matter involved a disciplinary proceeding resulting in part from the misuse of modern communications. But the use of technology and digital communications in law has continued to expand (LSO, "Technology"), and has a significant potential to affect bargaining process and outcomes (Roberts and Wright, 1491–93). The shift to formal use of online platforms, like Canada's first online forum at British Columbia's Civil Resolution Tribunal (CRT), is likely to continue. The need to understand how to effectively use technology, and to appreciate when others may not be doing so, makes this aspect of "technical competency" an important part of being able to negotiate across differences.

When people communicate online, a lot of what is communicated is not readily discernable since it is not directly in-person. Much of human communication happens at a level that is not expressed in words and occurs through things like body language. This can include things like eye contact, gestures, and body movements. Nonverbal communication also includes what is known as **paralanguage** (McKay *et al.*), which consists of the tone, pacing, and level of speaking. We all engage in nonverbal communication, although we often do so at an unconscious level, and do not mindfully choose the messages we are putting forward nonverbally in many circumstances.

An important difference between textual communications and the use of video to facilitate negotiations is that video provides some opportunity to engage in reading nonverbal signs. This likely helps to decrease social distancing, which breaks down awareness of the other parties' context and emotions. Social distancing may in part explain why textual communications alone can be more disputatious, as discussed below. The less distant parties perceive themselves to be, the less they focus only on self-interest, and the more inclined they are to collaborative behaviours. In contrast to email or text, video presents both auditory and visual cues, providing for better reading of nonverbal behaviours (Ebner, 155).

While video has the potential to improve adverse effects due to social distancing, it also has some additional potential pitfalls. Challenges in video negotiations might include decreased eye contact, limited screen scope, choppy transmission, the effects of lighting, or other external distractors and audio quality (Ebner and Thompson). Even so, these kinds of social and technical challenges are likely exacerbated through even less direct textual communications. In one study of police negotiators, for example, the increased use of texts to defuse violent situations has led some to observe that textual negotiation likely warrants specialized training (Almond and Budden; Roberts and Wright, 1492).

Negotiating through email, for example, presents several known and suspected challenges. The proliferation of the smartphone in the last decade means that people are no longer bound physically to their desktops and can now read and respond anywhere "synchronously" using both email and text (Ebner, 2014). Text messaging in particular is a new innovation about which relatively little is known in negotiations (Roberts and Wright, 1492). Research on email, though, suggests that these textual processes have potential to be contentious with less integrative outcomes; a diminishment of trust, privacy, and focus; and the potential to increase fundamental attributions (Ebner).[9]

For example, email and text readers sometimes "cherry pick," or selectively choose parts of the conversation to respond to (Ebner, 120), and then use them to argue their positions are "right," rather than working collaboratively. Some have concluded that email may therefore exacerbate competitive behaviours (Bhappu and Barsness). However, note that the indirect nature of email also has potential advantages, since it may lessen perception of things like cultural differences, which has the potential salutary effect of reducing the influence of unconscious biases in communications (Ebner, 119–120). Part of the strategizing for negotiations should therefore include a consideration of how communications will occur to maximize their utility for clients.

Ultimately, given the ubiquity of communications devices, bargainers should be as conscious as possible with respect to the risks and benefits of different mediums, since their use in some form seems increasingly inevitable with technological change. Some further suggestions about navigating differences arising from culture and technology are addressed in the next sections on building rapport and enhancing communication across differences.

ESTABLISHING AND BUILDING RAPPORT

Rapport is the development of a connection with someone such that the parties feel that they "click" or understand one another. Professional rapport involves mutual attentiveness, focus, and clear communication. Operating with integrity and having reliably strong professional ethics, as discussed earlier in this chapter, is an excellent way to establish long-term professional relationships with colleagues and staff. Further, the negotiation strategies involved in win-win, interest-based negotiation, as discussed in Chapter 1, are directed at an endgame of establishing positive, mutually beneficial relationships between counterparts. Thus, negotiation skills and strong professional ethics are among the most significant ways to establish rapport. Yes, "soft skills" are important, but lawyers are professionals, and your reputation in the community for being reliable and collegial, and predictably working towards interest-based win-win solutions are the best tool you have in the long term for establishing rapport.

Having said that, there are some behavioural skills and techniques that can help a negotiator develop rapport in the moment. These are thematically connected by expectations and attentiveness. In our experience, dressing appropriately is a good first step to cultivate a positive first impression to build rapport. Our observation likely leverages another cognitive bias—the halo effect—where others make judgements and attribute positive values based on things like appearance.[10] Bargainers should, however, also be aware that the effect can sometimes work in reverse, with negative characteristics being presumed. In this respect, some "norms" within a group may be different from others, and acceptable departures can be difficult to determine—what is "appropriate" in an unequal and culturally diverse social world may be complicated. At its simplest though, it's important to acknowledge that others may be put more at ease by dealing with someone whose actions and looks fit generally accepted role expectations.

It is really simple, but good advice to "remember that a person's name is, to that person, the sweetest and most important sound in any language" (Carnegie, 73). Learning and remembering people's names is another great way to establish rapport. As another bit of anecdotal advice, people very rarely misstep by being overly formal in addressing others in law, perhaps because tradition is so deeply embedded in legal culture. It's a good practice to always use appropriate titles or honourifics when addressing others, even in what might ostensibly be private communications like an email. As one BC case of lawyer professional misconduct shows, even not using the title "Mr." could be considered disrespectful, and in that matter contributed to what was the sanctionable professional misconduct of the lawyer (*Harding*, para 89).

It might also be useful to take some notes about other bargaining participants, to remember details about them from case to case to foster familiarity in order to build professional trust. These techniques, including possibly sharing some personal information, shared language, geographical and cultural references, all serve to "unmask" the participants in a negotiation, creating bonds that build trust and create rapport. In textual communications, these methods may be especially useful to reduce anonymity and sense of distance and can be combined with things like preliminary email and socially oriented contact, even before bargaining formally begins (Nadler and Shestowsky).

As we noted in Chapter 2, "mirroring" can also help to build rapport in bargaining sessions. Watch body language in direct or video negotiations. In all situations, but especially in the context of written negotiations, be especially mindful of word choices and apparent tone, or how what you write might be perceived. Reinforcing some behaviours and attitudes by reflecting them back can be useful in building nonverbal rapport. Adopt a similar level of energy and temperament, to the extent that it feels comfortable.

Don't overdo mirroring as, in our experience, it comes across—and will actually *be*—inauthentic. To make it simpler, just try conveying some level of genuine interest in your counterpart. Being overly familiar can also lead to other challenges, such as when bargainers attempt to employ humour; if received well, humour can help in negotiations, and break tension (Krishnan *et al.*). However, limits to online communication mean tone and nuance may be lost in negotiations. People may overestimate how clear they are being in communications, and even at the best of times, subtler connotations like sarcasm and wryness can be interpreted incorrectly (Kruger *et al.*). Either online or in-person, when combined with sensitivities based on differences like social context and culture, jokes can easily be misunderstood or misinterpreted (Ebner, 126).

EFFECTIVE COMMUNICATION ACROSS DIFFERENCES

As discussed in Chapter 1, negotiation is a kind of conversation. Even if it is conducted in writing, it is a form of interpersonal communication. The parties to a negotiation are fundamentally involved in the exchange of messages. A party that can effectively convey to their counterpart their position and their interests is far more likely to have those interests served by the negotiation. Basic skills and techniques for strong communication can therefore help negotiators immensely in being more effective at achieving the results that meet their interests and those of their clients.

Knowing one's own limitations, and the limitations on the potential of a particular communication for being effective, is also important. In addition to role, culture, and technical differences, legal services providers can be important conduits for directing clients experiencing language issues or communications-related disabilities by providing members of the public with information, referrals, and services that may be available in an accessible linguistic format, which might include the use of interpreters or interpretation services.

There is no "one size fits all" approach for how to interact with others, but courtesy, civility, and respect are core to the ethical obligations of all integrative negotiators and a significant way to build a reputation for professionalism in bargaining. Building on the strategies for good negotiators set out at the end of the last chapter, the following are some additional general techniques that can further assist in bargaining across individual differences, social context and culture, and in online interactions.

Find out about the Participants and Negotiators in Advance

In addition to going through the seven steps approach recommended in Chapter 1, it is recommended that negotiators also spend time learning about their counterparts to the extent it is possible to do so before a negotiation takes place.

It is also crucial to be attentive to how one communicates with court staff and administrators, as well as other participants in criminal law resolution discussions. Developing working relationships with everyone involved in resolution discussions can help make individual negotiations function better and serve to build both reputation and skills to better assist clients. As suggested in our discussion of online negotiations, some social interaction, or "unmasking," including limited personal disclosure, can help humanize the process and build empathy and rapport in all contexts.

Actively Listen

The capacity for multi-tasking in negotiations is often overestimated and, particularly in regard to technologies like smartphones, may be detrimental (Kurtzberg *et al.*). In addition, a good approach and strategy can help bargainers to respond in the moment. Do not waste your opportunity to hear and process your counterpart's interests by filling your mind with what you plan to say next when they are speaking. Focus on what they are saying, clearly articulate that you want to have a correct understanding of what they are communicating, and confirm it by repeating paraphrases back to them, using phrases like, "I think what you are saying is …" or "let me know if I am wrong: my understanding of what you just said is …"

Be Curious

Be open when negotiating and turn your mind to the effects of differences when asking open-ended questions. Consider what you don't know about the other party's interests. Try to learn more about them. Allocate a sufficient amount of time for the conversation to allow exploration of unanticipated terrains. Even if these are tangential, they can build rapport and provide clues about the party's interests and concerns, which may prove to be highly relevant to discovering win-win paths forward.

Use Silences

People often feel compelled to fill all the space in a conversation, especially when they are nervous. Avoid this. Be prepared to deliberately leave silences in direct negotiations. Pause to breathe before speaking. Ask "what do you think," and then pause to allow the counterpart to answer. Silence can be productive; it opens up a space for the other party to speak, and for you to gather information about differences and to learn more about specific interests.

In written communications, emails, and texts, consciously plan to vary the pace at which you respond. Read messages more than once and consider delaying hasty responses. Consider also that the prevalence of connective technology lends itself to immediate, and not always very fully thought out, replies, which may be limited in the number of textual characters. As one commentator notes, "the fact that you can now answer instantly in more cases than ever before doesn't mean that you should!" (Ebner, 121). Put another way and to adapt a currently popular meme on social media, which contains a pearl of wisdom, "dance like no one is watching, but email and text like it might one day be read aloud in court."

Be Concise

Plan ahead on the important points or information that you anticipate will need to be clearest and most direct. Try to spend more time listening than talking. Respect the other party's intelligence. When you do speak, use plain language rather than complex terminology, and repeat what others say, as both confirmation and perception checks to clarify communications. Prepare by organizing what you plan to say beforehand into sets of two or three main points. Practice your "elevator pitch"—as if you have only the time of an elevator ride to make your case; in a few sentences, summarize your most persuasive point or "bottom line" and, briefly, the arguments and evidence that support your position.

SUMMARY

This chapter examined differences that can affect criminal law bargaining, based on the role of the Crown and defence, social context and culture, and using technology in negotiations. The adversarial nature of criminal law, its dispute over fundamental rights and the public role of the prosecution mean that appreciating the different functions of either side in criminal law negotiations is imperative. The examination of the Donald Marshall case illustrated the risks in criminal procedure when the different roles of Crown and defence function ineffectively.

The case study also served as a departure point for discussion of the effects of social and cultural differences, which highlighted the differential treatment of Indigenous peoples by Canada's criminal justice system. The significance of procedures to address social and cultural differences set out in the *Criminal Code*, like *Gladue* reports, was also the further subject of a scenario involving the application of these principles in a practical situation.

We also built on our earlier discussion of theories and integrative styles to present specific consideration of social and cultural differences, and those that can arise procedurally as a result of the increasing ubiquity of online bargaining, and some potential implications of digital negotiations using video, email, and text. We ended our look at negotiating across differences by presenting some techniques for building rapport, and intentionally enhancing communication strategies to anticipate and improve modern bargaining across differences. In the next chapter, we extend our examination of differences in criminal law bargaining through an assessment of the role and place of other related ADR approaches, as well as special issues arising in the context of victims' rights and questions about capacity.

SUGGESTIONS FOR FURTHER READING

Banks, R. Richard, Jennifer L. Eberhardt, and Lee Ross. "Discrimination and Implicit Bias in a Racially Unequal Society." (2006) 94 *Calif L R* 1169.

Bhabha, Faisal. "*R v NS*: What's Fair in a Trial? The Supreme Court of Canada's Divided Decision on the Niqab in the Courtroom." (2014) 75 *Osgoode Legal Studies Research Paper Series*. <http://digitalcommons. osgoode.yorku.ca/olsrps/75>.

Carling, Amanda. "A Way to Reduce Indigenous Overrepresentation: Prevent False Guilty Plea Wrongful Convictions." (2017) 64 *CLQ* 415.

Craver, Charles. "Do Alternative Dispute Resolution Procedures Disadvantage Women and Minorities?" (2017) 70 *SMU L Rev* 891.

Demers, Annette. "Cultural Competence and the Legal Profession: An Annotated Bibliography of Materials Published between 2000 and 2011." (2011) 39 *Int'l J Legal Info* 22.

Eltis, Karen. *Courts, Litigants and the Digital Age*, 2nd ed. Toronto: Irwin Law, 2016.

Fiss, Owen. "Against Settlement." (1984) 93 *Yale L J* 1073.

House of Commons. *Indigenous People in the Federal Correctional System: Report of the Standing Committee on Public Safety and National Security*. Ottawa: Publications Canada, 2018. <http://publications.gc.ca/collections/collection_2018/parl/xc76-1/XC76-1-1-421-22-eng.pdf>. Accessed February 20, 2019.

Pay, Cynthia. "Teaching Cultural Competency in Legal Clinics." (2014) 23 *J L Law & Soc Pol'y* 188–219.

Salyzyn, Amy. "Courtroom Technology Competence as a Lawyer's Ethical Duty: What Should Regulators Do About It?" in Karim Benyekhlef, Jane Bailey, Jacuelyn Burkell, and Fabien Gelinas, editors, *eAccess to Justice*. Ottawa: University of Ottawa Press, 2016.

Schneider, Andrea Kupfer. "Negotiating While Female." (2017) 70 *SMU L Rev* 695.

Truth and Reconciliation Commission of Canada. *Honouring the Truth, Reconciling for the Future: Summary of the Final Report of the Truth and Reconciliation Commission of Canada*. Ottawa: Truth and Reconciliation Commission of Canada, 2015. <http://www.trc.ca/index.html>.

ENDNOTES

1.   Though some note the argument that "cultural competence is implicit in Rule 2.1 (Integrity) and Rule 6.3 (Harassment and Discrimination) of the *Model Code*," see Woolley *et al.*, eds., 2017, 189, and discussion at 188–208.

2.   Advocates' Society, *Guide*, 57. The question of using demeanour to assess legal credibility, and question of the of limits cultural accommodations

have continued to challenge courts. See Faisal Bhabha, "*R v NS*: What's Fair in a Trial? The Supreme Court of Canada's Divided Decision on the Niqab in the Courtroom," which examines the Supreme Court of Canada's 2012 decision related to the traditional right to full answer and defence or to "face" accusers in the justice system, while accommodating a witness who wished to remain veiled.

3.   Named after the case that interpreted the provision in *R v Gladue*, [1999] 1 SCR, 688, CanLII 679, that was affirmed and expanded in the 2012 decision in *R v Ipeelee* 2012; quotation at para 60.

4.   "Manifestations of this injustice include over- and under-policing, discriminatory bail, trial and sentencing outcomes, and mass incarceration"; see Tanovich at 656.

5.   The preparation of *Gladue* reports may require special knowledge, expertise, and assistance; see Clarke *et al.*

6.   Andrew-Gee reports on a 2017 Statistics Canada national crime survey that tracked the rate of attrition of sexual assault allegations, showing that only 20 percent of the claims that make it into the system go to court.

7.   Which has recently led to calls for imposition of mandatory judicial education through legislation (Harrison).

8.   Jolls and Sunstein, who note at 975 that implicit bias often results from the first of two cognitive systems, which is "rapid, intuitive and error prone."

9.   Ebner also notes, in the "Seven Major Challenges" of email negotiation, that email may diminish negotiator commitment and investment, at 119.

10.   First noted by Edward Thorndike.

REFERENCES

Advocates' Society. *Guide for Lawyers Working with Indigenous Peoples.* February 28, 2018. <https://www.advocates.ca/Upload/Files/PDF/ Advocacy/BestPracticesPublications/Guide_for_Lawyers_Working_ with_Indigenous_Peoples_may16.pdf>. Accessed February 19, 2019.

Almond, Louise, and Marc Budden. "The Use of Text Messages Within a Crisis Negotiation: Help or Hinderance?" (2012) 12:1 *Police Crisis Negots* 1.

Andrew-Gee, Eric. "One in Five Sexual-Assault Cases Go to Court, Study Finds." *Globe and Mail*, 2017, October 26.

Bhabha, Faisal. "*R v NS*: What's Fair in a Trial? The Supreme Court of Canada's Divided Decision on the Niqab in the Courtroom." (2014) 75 *Osgoode Legal Studies Research Paper Series*. <http://digitalcommons. osgoode.yorku.ca/olsrps/75>.

Bhappu, A. D., and Z. I. Barsness. "Risks of Email," in A. K. Schneider and C. Honeyman, editors, *The Negotiator's Fieldbook: The Desk Reference for the Experienced Negotiator*. Washington, DC: American Bar Association, 2006.

Blair, I., J. Ma, and A. Lenton. "Imagining Stereotypes Away: The Moderation of Implicit Stereotypes through Mental Imagery." (2001) 81 *Journal of Personality and Social Psychology* 828–841.

Boucher v The Queen [1955] SCR 16.

Bryant, Sue. "The Five Habits: Building Cross-Cultural Competence in Lawyers." (2001) 8 *Clinical L Rev* 33.

Carnegie, Dale. *How to Win Friends and Influence People*. New York: Gallery, 1998.

Casey, P. M., R. K. Warren, F. L. Cheesman, and J. K. Elek. *Helping Courts Address Implicit Bias*. Williamsburg, VA: National Center for State Courts, 2012.

Civil Resolution Tribunal (CRT). Province of British Columbia. <https:// civilresolutionbc.ca/>. Accessed April 12, 2019.

Clarke, Judy, Jennifer Hepburn, and Carol Herter, editors. *Gladue Report Guide*. Victoria, BC: Legal Services Society, BC, 2018. <http://www. bcrb.bc.ca/Gladue-Report-Guide-eng.pdf>. Accessed June 12, 2019.

Craig, Elaine. "The Ethical Obligations of Defence Counsel in Sexual Assault Cases." (2014) 51:2 *Osgoode Hall L J* 427.

Criminal Code of Canada RSC 1985, c, C-46 [*Criminal Code*].

Deardorff, D. K. *The Sage Handbook of Intercultural Competence*. Thousand Oaks, CA: Sage, 2009.

Dodek, Adam. "Lawyering at the Intersection of Public Law and Legal Ethics: Government Lawyers as Custodians of the Rule of Law." (2010) 33 *Dal L J* 1.

Doolittle, Robin. "Unfounded: Why Police Dismiss 1 in 5 Sexual Assault Claims as Baseless." *Globe and Mail*, 2017, February 3.

Dripps, Donald A. "Fundamental Retribution Error: Criminal Justice and the Social Psychology of Blame." (2003) 56 *Van L Rev* 1383.

Ebner, Noam. "Negotiating via Email," in C. Honeyman and
A. K. Schneider, editors, *The Negotiator's Desk Reference*. St. Paul, MN:
DRI Press, 2017.

Ebner, Noam, and T. Thompson. "@ Face Value? Nonverbal Communication
and Trust Development in Online Video-Based Mediation." (2014) 2
Int'l J Online Disp Resol.

Federation of Law Societies. *Model Code of Professional Conduct* [FLSC,
Model Code], as amended March 14, 2017. <https://flsc.ca/wp-content/
uploads/2018/03/Model-Code-as-amended-March-2017-Final.pdf>.
Accessed January 20, 2019.

Galinsky, A., and G. Moskowitz. "Perspective-Taking: Decreasing
Stereotype Expression, Stereotype Accessibility, and In-Group
Favoritism." (2010) 78 *J Pers Soc Psychol* 702–724.

Ghittens, Margaret, and David Cole. *Report of the Commission on Systemic
Racism in the Ontario Criminal Justice System*. Ottawa: Queen's Printer for
Ontario, 1995.

Hall, Stuart. "Cultural Studies: Two Paradigms." (1980) 2 *Media Cult Soc*
57–72.

Harding (Re), 2013 LS BC 25 CanLII.

Harrison, Thomas. "Judicial Education Doesn't Breach Independence,
but Bill C-337 Might." *IRPP-Policy Options*, 2017, May 22. <http://
policyoptions.irpp.org/magazines/may-2017/judicial-education-doesnt-
breach-independence-but-bill-c-337-might/>. Accessed November 4,
2017.

Hartley, James. "Note-taking in Non-academic Settings: A Review." (2002)
16:5 *Applied Cognitive Psychology*.

Jolls, Christine, and Sunstein, Cass R. "The Law of Implicit Bias." (2006)
Faculty Scholarship Series. Paper 1824. <http://digitalcommons.law.yale.
edu/fss_papers/1824>.

Krishnan, Aparna, Terri R. Kurtzberg, and Charles E. Naquin. "The Curse
of the Smartphone: Electronic Multitasking in Online Negotiations."
(2014) 30:2 *Negotiation Journal* 198.

Kruger, Justin, Nicholas Epley, Jason Parker, and Zhi-Wen Ng.
"Egocentrism Over E-Mail: Can We Communicate as Well as We
Think?" (2005) 89:6 *J Pers Soc Psychol* 925.

Kurtzberg, Terri R., Charles E. Naquin, and Liuba Y. Belkin. "Humour as a Relation-Building Tool in Online Negotiations." (2009) 20:4 *Int J Confl Manage* 377.

Law Society of Ontario (LSO). *Statement of Principles.* 2018. <https://lso.ca/about-lso/initiatives/edi/statement-of-principles>. Accessed February 20, 2019.

Law Society of Ontario (LSO). *Equity, Diversity and Inclusion.* 2019. <https://lso.ca/about-lso/initiatives/edi>. Accessed February 20, 2019.

Law Society of Ontario (LSO). "Technology," in *Practice Management Guidelines.* <https://lso.ca/lawyers/practice-supports-and-resources/practice-management-guidelines>. Accessed February 21, 2019.

Luban, David. "Settlements and the Erosion of the Public Realm." (1985) 85:2619 *Georgetown L Rev* 2659–2662.

Malakieh, Jamil. *Adult and Youth Correctional Statistics in Canada, 2016/2017.* Ottawa: Statistics Canada, 2018. <http://publications.gc.ca/collections/collection_2018/parl/xc76-1/XC76-1-1-421-22-eng.pdf>. Accessed February 20, 2019.

McKay, Matthew, Martha Davis, and Patrick Fanning. *Messages: The Communication Skills Book*, 2nd ed. Oakland, CA: New Harbinger Publications, 1995.

Mezey, Naomi. "Law as Culture." (2001) 13 *Yale J L & Human* 35–67.

Nadler, J., and D. Shestowsky. "Negotiation, Information Technology and the Problem of the Faceless Other," in L.L Thompson, editor, *Negotiation Theory and Research.* New York: Psychology Press, 2006.

National Association of Criminal Defense Attorneys (NACDL). *The Trial Penalty: The Sixth Amendment Right to Trial on the Verge of Extinction and How to Save It.* Washington, DC: NACDL, 2018. <www.nacdl.org/trialpenaltyreport>.

Oliver, Wesley MacNeil, and Rishi Batra. "Standards of Legitimacy in Criminal Negotiations." (2015) 20 *Harv Negot L R* 61.

Public Prosecution Service of Canada. *Deskbook* [PPSC, *Deskbook*]. <https://www.ppsc-sppc.gc.ca/eng/pub/fpsd-sfpg/fps-sfp/tpd/p3/ch07.html>. Accessed January 20, 2019.

R v Anthony-Cook, 2016 SCC 43 CanLII.

R v Gladue, (1999) 679 CanLII (SCC); [1999] 1 SCR 688 [*Gladue*].

R v Ipeelee, [2012] SCC 13 (CanLII); 1 SCR 433 [*Ipeelee*].

R v McIlvride-Lister, (2019) ONSC 1869 CanLII [*McIlvride-Lister*].

R v SK (RD), [1997] 3 SCR 484.

Roberts, Jenny, and Ronald F. Wright. "Training for Bargaining." (2016) 57 *Wm & Mary L Rev* 1445.

Royal Commission on the Donald Marshall, Jr., Prosecution Digest of Findings and Recommendations. 1989 [*Marshall Inquiry*].

Seligman, Martin E. P., Paul R. Verkuil, and Terry H. Kang. "Why Lawyers Are Unhappy." (2001) 23 *Cardozo L Rev* 52.

Sherrin, Chris. "Guilty Pleas from the Innocent." (2011) 30:1 *Windsor Rev Leg Soc* 8–9.

Statistics Canada. "Adult Correctional Statistics in Canada, 2015/2016." Ottawa: Statistics Canada, 2016.

Strub, T., and B. McKimmie. "Note Takers Who Review Are Less Vulnerable to the Influence of Stereotypes than Note Takers Who Do Not Review." (2012) 18 *Psychol Crime Law* 859–876.

Tanovich, David. "The Charter of Whiteness: Twenty-Five Years of Maintaining Racial Injustice in the Canadian Criminal Justice System." (2008) 40 *SCLR* (2d) 655.

Thorndike, E. L. "A Constant Error in Psychological Rating." (1920) 4 *J Appl Psychol* 25–29.

Truth and Reconciliation Commission of Canada (TRC). *Truth and Reconciliation Commission of Canada: Calls to Action Report*. Ottawa: Truth and Reconciliation Commission, 2015.

Voyvodic, Rose. "Lawyers Meet the Social Context: Understanding Cultural Competence." (2005) 84 *Can Bar Rev* 563.

Woolley, A., Richard F. Devlin, Brent Cotter, and John M. Law, editors. *Lawyers' Ethics and Professional Regulation*, 3rd ed. Toronto: LexisNexis, 2017.

PART II

Alternative Approaches in Canadian Criminal Law

CHAPTER 4

Alternative Dispute Resolution (ADR) and Diversion in Criminal Law

LEARNING OBJECTIVES

After reading this chapter, in relation to criminal law, students should:

- Understand alternative dispute resolution (ADR) processes like mediation and arbitration
- Appreciate the ethical obligations of ADR professionals
- Know diversionary alternatives to prosecution, including for youth criminals and those with diminished capacity
- Develop insight into the purpose and function of victim-offender mediation
- Have familiarity with ADR in family law cases involving criminal violence
- Internalize some practical guidance for engaging professionally in ADR processes in Canada

OVERVIEW

The first part of this text emphasized personal approach, style, and strategies, along with professional competencies and skills that can be cultivated by lawyers and other legal services professionals seeking to effectively resolve conflicts. In Part II, we focus less on individual skills and more on broader systems and processes related to negotiation in criminal law. Though most think of criminal law as the adversarial clash of words and arguments in a formal trial proceeding, as we have seen in the first few chapters, the vast majority of proceedings are in fact resolved through alternative means like negotiation.

However, in addition to bargaining, other ADR methods and diversionary mechanisms have also become incorporated within Canadian criminal justice. This chapter highlights alternative processes related to negotiation, as well as highlighting alternatives to prosecution through the diversion of criminal law offenders. Restorative justice, a separate concept related to ADR, is given separate, more detailed consideration in Chapter 5.

Chapter 4 begins by briefly defining alternative dispute resolution (ADR). We situate alternatives to criminal litigation in the context of recent efforts to create options to trial proceedings throughout the legal system. We then discuss common forms of ADR that are employed in the criminal law context, with a particular emphasis on mediation and arbitration. The chapter then goes on to critically consider some of the special ethical implications and obligations of professionals participating in ADR and diversionary procedures.

ADR falls within a larger category of mechanisms that seek to divert some offenders into less formal, often community-based resolutions, prior to conviction. In our section on alternatives to prosecution, we examine some of the diversions that are used within criminal justice. Here, we show the nature of diversion generally, but also through a more detailed examination in relation to its role with youth criminals and those who may have capacity or mental health issues.

Next, we look at victim-offender mediation as one of the main ways that ADR is employed in criminal law, usually following a finding of guilt. The role of victim-offender mediation is illustrated in a recent Canadian case study that demonstrates the considerations involved in these procedures in criminal law. A further common use of ADR is in family law and child protection proceedings. Our penultimate section further considers the distinct issues arising in this area of law, where there are also sometimes criminal or family violence allegations, which require both caution and sometimes modification of alternative procedures. Finally, the chapter sets forth some brief practical guidance for legal professionals to effectively and ethically engage in ADR processes, which, though ancillary to criminal prosecution in court, are a substantive part of the Canadian criminal justice system.

ALTERNATIVE DISPUTE RESOLUTION IN CRIMINAL LAW

Alternative dispute resolution (ADR) is an umbrella term encompassing a variety of procedures. ADR is best understood as a spectrum of approaches adopted by parties voluntarily in place of or to complement court proceedings (Emond). ADR therefore functions within the more formal framework of traditional litigation in the justice system. There is a wide variety of alternative methods that parties can privately agree to employ as means to settle disagreements or disputes (MacFarlane).

Recognized ADR procedures involve variations in collaborative resolution approaches that include negotiation, but also mediation, arbitration, and hybrids like mediation-arbitration. Mediation is a process, typically out of court and less formal than regular litigation, where an independent third party is brought in to help participants proactively settle their disputes. Similarly, arbitration also usually occurs outside court, where parties agree to be bound by the decision of an independent decision-maker. In the criminal context, ADR can also refer to restorative justice practices and other forms of community-engaged justice. Generally, over the last several decades modern approaches to ADR have been widely recognized and accepted by the legal system.[1]

Part of the reason ADR has become so ubiquitous is that in the civil context, involving private disputes between parties, it can be comparatively both more cost-effective and faster. As an aspect of access to justice and improving judicial economy, these processes also have potential to reduce the caseload faced by courts, to make more resources available in the administration of justice. Throughout the Canadian legal system, ADR processes like mediation have become so integrated that some argue their use has eclipsed traditional court procedures like trials (Bromwich and Harrison).[2]

The increasing use of ADR validates the observation of scholars, like Lon Fuller, that different processes may be better than adjudication in resolving some disputes, especially when the non-legal aspects of social conflicts may be important (Bush and Fulger *et al.*). A balanced assessment of ADR overall suggests it has some potential downsides, since putatively private settlements may not be as open to scrutiny and do not produce precedential jurisprudence in the same way as in the regular court system. Caution in the use of ADR in criminal law is also warranted given the need for transparency in the state's enforcement of public interests. As we've noted in previous chapters, a primary justification for adversarialism is based on the need to defend and enforce fundamental rights (Luban), and in criminal law there may be instances where this inherent dichotomy is both appropriate and unavoidable. Even in the best of circumstances, the capacity for the use of alternative procedures to resolve criminal matters may therefore be limited.

However, as in other areas of law, ADR's impact in criminal justice continues to grow. ADR allows for some of the benefits of legal processes, like confidentiality, while providing the opportunity for improved legal remedies. Since these approaches de-emphasize adversarialism, they also have the potential to better address matters where non-legal factors, like the ongoing relationships between parties, are important dimensions of the conflict.[3] While ADR is more often understood to apply specifically in the context of private law, a range of ADR options exist in the criminal law context, which often work in conjunction with diversionary procedures to provide a range of alternatives. As with negotiation, the use of different ADR approaches in criminal matters also raises specific ethical considerations for legal services professionals.

ADR AND ETHICS IN CRIMINAL LAW

Using ADR approaches to resolve criminal matters has implications for what constitutes ethical or "good" lawyering (Emond). As with the obligation to understand and demonstrate negotiation competencies discussed in Chapter 2, lawyers and legal services professionals have ethical duties when utilizing ADR, which may also be subject to regulatory scrutiny. Those involved in facilitating ADR must understand these procedures well enough to explain available options to clients, setting out the risks and benefits to choose an appropriate process. They should also be able to counsel clients about practical features of these alternatives, such as the optimal time for use of ADR, and be able as well to assist in the selection of an appropriately qualified neutral, like a mediator or arbitrator with experience and understanding of criminal law resolutions.

In Canadian criminal law, counsel have duties imposed by professional codes of conduct. In addition to specific negotiation competencies (FLSC, *Model Code*, 3.1-1 (v)), all lawyers must have the skills to implement ADR (FLSC, *Model Code*, 3.1-1 (v)). As we noted in Chapter 2, the professional rules are largely silent on exactly what ADR skills legal professionals require. Still, generally all lawyers are encouraged to compromise or settle disputes, where it is reasonable. In particular, "a lawyer should consider the use of alternative dispute resolution (ADR) when appropriate, inform the client of ADR options and, if so instructed, take steps to pursue those options" (FLSC, *Model Code*, 3.2-4, Commentary [1]). So, for example, in the criminal law context these regulatory duties capture the obligation to advise criminal defendants about the risks and benefits of ADR.

For their part, Crown Attorneys also have additional obligations imposed by legal regulators. These duties require prosecutors to consider the appropriateness of a variety of options in each case, including ADR and alternative diversions from criminal procedures. Obligations of the Crown are also often imposed by their prosecutorial service, like the Ministry of the Attorney General, and by legislation (Rosenberg). Crowns are required to act "justly" in the public interest, so their primary goal is not necessarily to seek either convictions or the highest penalty in criminal matters. In accordance with relevant legal provisions and ministerial guidance, part of the prosecutor's role is to assess the appropriateness of alternatives to prosecution and the use of ADR in criminal proceedings, both of which are examined in the next two sections.

DIVERSIONARY ALTERNATIVES TO PROSECUTION

Recognized ADR procedures in criminal law also work in tandem with an array of diversionary mechanisms. In appropriate circumstances, these diversions offer alternatives to prosecution and are supported by things like Crown policy guidelines. A directive related to Indigenous peoples produced by the Ontario Attorney General's office, for example, explicitly reinforces emerging recognitions about Canada's First Nations and "require[s] consideration of the unique circumstances of Indigenous Peoples" (Ministry of the Attorney General). More generally though, Ontario Crowns may also exercise their prosecutorial discretion to use alternative community justice programs to address criminal conduct. Where no such programs exist, prosecutors are guided under the "Community Justice Program for Adults" to exercise broad authority "to consider informal modes of diversion," citing, as an example, a donation to charity (Ministry of the Attorney General).

Legislation may also provide for diversion from formal proceedings in other areas of criminal law. For example, Section 4 of the federal *Youth Criminal Justice Act* (YCJA) notes that "extrajudicial sanctions" (EJS) are "often the most appropriate and effective way to address youth crime." For juvenile offenders, the YCJA also recognizes that in some cases simple warnings and cautions by police before the start of proceedings may be warranted and effective (YCJA, ss 6–8). Where matters proceed more formally, the law also permits the imposition of EJS in certain situations, which can lead to the dismissal of criminal charges that otherwise would have had a reasonable prospect of conviction if tried (YCJA, s 10 (1)–(5)).

As suggested earlier in the example of criminal allegations against Indigenous persons, legislative imperatives typically work complementarily with things like local prosecution policy. In looking at the YCJA, Ontario Crowns are guided by directions which highlight the EJS provisions for youth. These directions note, for example, "the principles of the YCJA require that the criminal justice system for young persons be distinct from that of adults and must acknowledge a presumption of diminished moral blameworthiness or culpability for youth."[4]

Similarly, community-based sanctions may be an alternative in other situations, such as where mental health and capacity are an issue in criminal proceedings. Typically, more serious allegations, such as murder and offences involving firearms, terrorism, and robbery,[5] are not subject to alternatives and diversion from prosecution. The question of mental health or the capacity of the parties is a challenge that raises at least three more issues, all of which touch on ADR and diversion in criminal law proceedings, that all legal services professionals should know.

First, the common law generally presumes that people have the capacity to act, and make independent decisions.[6] For lawyers, there is also a professional presumption that clients have the ability to give directions. However, where a client may lack or have diminished capacity, advocates may have special responsibilities under applicable professional rules (FLSC, *Model Code*, 3.2-9). The *Criminal Code* sets out a similar expectation that individuals are presumed to be fit to participate in formal proceedings like trials (*Criminal Code*, s 672.22), but the assessment of individual capacity may also be an issue that requires monitoring throughout proceedings (FLSC, *Model Code*, 3.2-9, Commentary [3]).

A second capacity issue that may involve ADR and diversion involves the prosecution side of criminal matters. Where the cognitive ability or mental health of an individual is a factor in an alleged crime, prosecutors can consider a wide range of medical, psychological, and social factors about the accused. The circumstances, nature of an offence, and administration of justice considerations like the public confidence are factors that can affect both the process of criminal proceedings, and the outcomes in cases as noted further below.[7] Some jurisdictions provide for alternatives to prosecution that may include community-based programs to hold offenders accountable, but also seek to meet rehabilitative needs, provide for medication and psychiatric care, as well as to address non-medical issues like "good housing" and "proper ongoing support in the community" (*Crown Prosecution Manual*, s 26 (a)).

In terms of the results of criminal proceedings, the third main issue with respect to capacity and criminal law is a determination that someone is "not criminally responsible" for all or some of their criminal actions. Such findings typically occur following more formal proceedings, and reduce the individual culpability for criminal conduct on account of mental illness (*Criminal Code*, s 672.34). The potential for such findings will likely affect considerations in determining what, if any, criminal penalties should apply, and other alternative dispositions intended to address the incapacity or mental health issue that has been recognized by the court.

While community-based sanctions and alternatives to prosecution are one diversionary mechanism present in Canada's criminal justice system, more explicit alternative dispute resolution processes are frequently used in criminal justice. One prominent example of the use of ADR is through mediation between victims and perpetrators of crimes, addressed in the next section.

VICTIM-OFFENDER MEDIATION

Bargaining in criminal law often complements other ADR approaches like mediation and arbitration. One of the more prominent uses of ADR in recent years is through victim-offender mediation. This form of mediation is a voluntary, confidential process, in the course of which parties are assisted in their dialogue by a third-party neutral (Bush and Folger). The neutral mediator helps the parties communicate constructively and brainstorm possible solutions, ideally assisting them to arrive at a solution they are willing to settle on. The mediator does not impose resolution, but rather helps the parties come up with their own way of addressing their dispute. The mediation process affords an opportunity for participants to have a conversation about their conflict and to look at it in new ways. While ADR in criminal law can involve legal concepts and remedies like restitution, victim-offender mediation also usually seeks to address non-legal aspects of a crime, like the personal, psychological, and social impacts of the misconduct.

Victim-offender mediation bears conceptual similarities to other types of ADR as a kind of facilitated negotiation. However, it differs in some important ways. Parties involved in victim-offender mediation are not "disputants" (Umbreit, *Handbook*). The accused has clearly committed a criminal offence. In order to participate in the mediation, an accused must have admitted some level of responsibility for the harm caused. In this sense, victim-offender mediation is not a substitute for procedures to determine guilt for criminal acts.

Unlike other forms of mediation, where the perspectives of each party might be given equal consideration, the victim in these kinds of mediation has to be acknowledged as having endured an unmistakably criminal harm. As a result, the main goals of victim-offender mediation do not involve an expectation that settlement will represent a compromise between the divergent views of the parties. Instead, victim-offender mediation focuses more on dialogue than on settlement, seeking to emphasize what is required for victims to heal, offenders to be accountable for their wrongdoing, and losses to be mitigated or restored (Umbreit, *Handbook*).

While the field of mediating conflicts in criminal law is usually referred to as victim-offender mediation, it is sometimes also called "victim-offender reconciliation" (Umbreit, *Handbook*). No matter the label, studies have consistently shown high levels of party satisfaction with the outcomes of victim-offender mediation (*ibid*). While not everyone who has been victimized by crime will choose to participate in victim-offender mediation, and some may even oppose it in favour of the retributive goals of criminal justice (Umbreit, "Mediation"), many find it advantageous to do so.

Why might victims and offenders choose to participate in mediation? In the criminal justice system, the formal role of victims and others affected by crime is usually limited. They are not parties, since the state primarily treats crimes as contrary to the public interest. In this respect, the informational and emotional needs of victims, their friends and family, and others affected adversely by the process, like witnesses, may be left largely unaddressed (Umbreit, "Mediation"). By contrast, mediation permits victims, who otherwise do not have legal standing, to have a voice in matters where some parts of the criminal harm they have experienced can be addressed.

Through mediation, victims of crime, their family members, and affected witnesses can glean information, show offenders the impact of their crimes, and have a human face-to-face interaction with an offender, providing them a chance to personally hold the offender accountable for their crimes. Many participants in victim-offender mediation report that they are able to advance their own healing, feel heard, and sometimes reach a point where they are able to use the process to express forgiveness.

Most victim-offender mediation processes involve four phases:

1. Referral and case intake: Parties are identified and a program determines whether it is willing to investigate mediating a particular conflict.

2. Preparation for mediation: Generally, a mediator will first meet with each party separately at some time (often a week or so) before the scheduled mediation session. The mediator will ask the parties to relate their narratives of what happened. Usually, the mediator will also explain the program, particularly emphasizing that it is voluntary, invite them to participate, and prepare them for the meeting. This preliminary phase ensures that both parties provide informed consent to the mediation.

3. Mediation: This is the actual conversation between the parties. The mediator will engage in a process of seeking to understand the parties' positions and interests while facilitating their ability to communicate their views to one another. Then, the mediator will assist the parties in considering possible ways forward to address their interests within the framework provided by the criminal law. It may or may not be interrupted by pauses for "caucusing," in which the mediator meets separately with each party.

4. Follow-up: Generally, mediation programs will follow up with parties who have participated in victim-offender mediation at least once, and perhaps several times after the mediation is completed. It may be that a settlement is piloted, meaning that the parties expect to come back at least once or periodically to review how things are going and revisit or revise an agreement.

CASE STUDY: Victim-Offender Mediation

The following true case study of victim-offender mediation was taken directly from the website of the Canadian Community Justice Initiatives Association (CCJIA); pseudonyms have been used to protect the identities of persons involved.

"Ann" was one of a number of children whose father, a police officer, was murdered in the line of duty by two men whom he had pulled over on the highway. Ann and her siblings had adored their father and were devastated by his loss to them, to their mother, and to their community. As in far too many cases, while the people responsible were arrested and sent to prison, the needs not only went on, but magnified, over time. Ann is very open about what transpired in the aftermath of her father's killing: anesthetizing the pain led to years of addiction, downward spiral, despair, and dysfunction.

Many years had passed when "Charles" one of the men responsible for her father's death contacted us (CCJIA) through his institutional parole officer. Charles had heard from another inmate who had met with the family survivors harmed by the commission of his own crime that it had been an astonishing experience, one he would recommend to others. That began a time in which we visited with Charles from time to time to try to discern together whether or not to attempt to reach the victims/ survivors in his case. Charles was torn between wanting to share with them the depth of his sorrow for having taken their father's life, and wanting to avoid the possibility of re-traumatizing them with further contact, even by a sensitive third party. We made clear that, in the absence of any further information from the victims indicating interest in the process, we would not proceed until either he was more certain, or something new had transpired to indicate victim interest in the program.

Then, out of nowhere, Ann's brother wrote to us, unaware that we had been in conversation with Charles, saying he had been informed that Charles was incarcerated in our region, and wondering if we might be able to get a letter to him. We quickly responded to his letter by phone.

Continued

"This step," he explained, "is one I need to take toward my own healing: I've written a letter for Charles unconditionally granting forgiveness to him." He had come to the conviction, he said, that in order to be completely freed from the last vestiges of his addiction, he needed to forgive Charles, and finally rid himself of the remaining animosity, anger and desire for vengeance that he had used to justify his own substance abuse and long-term addiction. We promised to deliver his letter to Charles.

A few days later, we met with Charles, who sat quietly as he read the letter we had just handed him, slowly shaking his head in amazement at the words he was reading. He took the letter to his cell, read it a number of times daily, then composed a reply, finally able to express to one of the family members the depth of his sorrow and remorse for having taken their father's life, and ending with a profound statement of gratitude for the gift of forgiveness he had been given.

Within a few months, the next letter arrived from a member of the victim's family, this time from Ann. She had seen the impact on her brother of just the exchange of correspondence, and the new degree of freedom he exhibited. She wrote saying she wanted to write to Charles as well, but that she had hoped that an exchange of letters between them would culminate in an actual meeting: a face-to-face dialogue which VOMP (Victim Offender Mediation Program) staff would facilitate. Charles needed some time to get his head around that notion, meeting with the institutional Elder and praying about it together. It didn't take long before he asked us to set the meeting up, saying just the prospect of meeting with her had him almost overwhelmed with emotion at times, not certain what he could ever say that would be remotely adequate to the circumstance, yet hoping that whatever he might offer would help assuage her pain and increase a sense of peace for her.

At the end of March, Ann flew into Abbotsford, where we met her and spent some additional time with her to help prepare her for what the following day's meeting might bring. For two hours the next morning and two more in the afternoon these two met, sharing along a simple format: the past—the impact of the crime and its aftermath for both;

the present (what each was doing to heal and move on toward a more successful future); and the future: what hopes Charles held, given the length of sentence he had yet to serve, and what Ann hoped to accomplish, working with others, especially young women, from backgrounds and circumstances not dissimilar from her own. Toward the end of the afternoon, the institutional Elder, who had previously been invited, joined us. He commended both Charles and Ann for having done "this courageous thing," then, using the traditional drum that Charles had expertly painted with symbols deeply meaningful to Ann from her own Aboriginal tradition, the Elder sang a song befitting their meeting, shared deeply from his own heart, then prayed a prayer of thanksgiving, a celebration of the new degree of healing they had witnessed and safe travel for Ann.

In the next few weeks, we debriefed that encounter with both Ann and Charles. Ann told us she had written a letter to the Minister of Justice, believing that, as a woman of Aboriginal heritage, the Minister might just understand the deep healing of the spirit Ann was attempting to describe. She sent a copy of the letter to us, with permission to share it with others. This is what she wrote:

> Dear Minister of Justice,
>
> I am writing you this letter today in regards to a successful story of Fraser Region Community Justice Initiatives Association's Victim Offender Mediation (Restorative Justice) Program, Langley, British Columbia.
>
> My late father [a police officer] was gunned down in the line of duty [a number of years ago]. The offender is currently serving a life sentence in a prison in British Columbia. I had the chance to visit him in prison for a face-to-face meeting to help my healing process of this horrific loss in my life. This encounter took place on March 29, 2016. I believe this meeting to be history in the making.

Continued

I would like to thank you personally for having these programs in place so that families can take these opportunities to guide them in their healing process. I would like to commend the amazing work of Mr. Dave Gustafson and Susan Underwood, the two mediators that made this possible for myself to accomplish. Without the hard work that the staff do for this program, I would not have been able to take this path in my journey to heal and to guide the rest of my family towards this avenue.

The killing of my late father has been the hardest and most difficult thing to overcome; however no one (I believe) ever overcomes it. A person is able to forgive but never forgets. Two entirely different situations. I firmly believe in miracles as well, as the spirit world is in me, I feel it as I am an Aboriginal person. I was able to witness a miracle because I was able to forgive the offender and saw with my own eyes and heart that he truly was sorry and took full responsibility for his actions. Without the work of these mediators, the two of us (myself and the offender) would not have been able to meet one another for this very important event in our lives.

I could go on and on, however … all I need for you to know is that I came back home from this meeting with no hatred, anger or resentment in my heart whatsoever.

If you ever need a voice in the success of these stories, feel free to contact me. I will try to help other families find the closure they need, as I did. Once again, I would like for you to know that the VOMP Facilitators are angels from God. I cannot thank them enough for helping me in my journey to live happy, joyous and free.

Sincerely,

Ann

Case Study Discussion

Use the interest-based approach to ADR outlined in Chapter 1 to consider the interests of either side in the case study, and in particular, note the non-legal needs of the parties. There are a number of purposes for victim-offender mediation, including creating a forum for parties to get, or provide, further information about the crimes. One of the main purposes is to create a mechanism to help resolve emotional and other social needs, which may not be a focus of formal proceedings. What are some of the specific interests of the parties in the case study above that appear to fall into this latter category?

One possibility arising from victim-offender mediation is that offenders will apologize, be remorseful, or otherwise express regret. Psychologists acknowledge a number of potential benefits from saying "sorry" (Engel). This includes emotional healing and moving past negative emotions, like shame on the part of the perpetrator and anger on the part of victims and their family. The second part of apology is that sometimes it can create a degree of understanding and empathy for the wrongdoer. Appreciating the criminal's perspective can sometimes provoke compassion and lead to forgiveness. What are some of the reasons, in the case study or more generally, that parties would forgive someone who had committed a crime against them or someone they loved?

ADR AND FAMILY LAW VIOLENCE

Mediation and arbitration are commonly used to help settle family law disputes and in child protection. Like criminal law more generally, the majority of these family law cases are resolved without trials. Where family law and child protection matters also involve criminal violence, or abuse allegations, victims require special considerations when using ADR approaches (DOJ). In Chapter 2, we briefly discussed the phenomenon of increased challenges of threats and violence against officials in the formal justice system. One further aspect of this phenomenon arises in the context of violence and family law, potentially endangering both advocates acting to facilitate ADR, as well as the victims. One recent news headline announcing the fatal shooting deaths of an Arizona mediator and one of his clients following a mediation session underscores the fact that the dangers in this area of ADR are all too real.[8]

In these circumstances, mediators and arbitrators involved in both family and criminal law have particular obligations and face risks that should be taken "seriously" (Linton). For example, arbitrators working in family law in Ontario are required by law to take particular steps to screen for domestic violence to protect participants (*Arbitration Act*). There is a similar provision, requiring family dispute resolution professionals to assess the propriety of ADR, in British Columbia's legislation,[9] and courts have also formally recognized best practices in screening in family mediation and arbitration cases involving violence (*Wainwright*). Across Canada, there are a variety of legislative and institutional responses put in place to address this issue.[10]

In addition to legal obligations of practitioners, ADR professional bodies may also set standards to assess whether ADR processes are appropriate in family law cases involving violence. For example, as part of its "Safety Standards," the Ontario Association for Family Mediation (OAFM) assumes in its Policy on Intimate Partner Violence and Power Imbalances that "mediation of cases of Domestic Violence is probably inappropriate," and provides cautions about the need to be discerning about real or potential abuse. In this context, abuse is defined broadly in a non-exclusive list that includes objectionable conduct, some of which may also involve criminality:

1. physical violence, including assault;
2. sexual assault;
3. kidnapping, confining;
4. use of or threat with a weapon;
5. threats against children;
6. unlawful entry;
7. destruction or theft of personal property;
8. violence against pets;
9. stalking, harassment;

10. psychological and verbal abuse;
11. controlling and/or manipulative behaviour;
12. withholding of economic and other resources; and
13. penalizing the abused person for asserting his/her independence or autonomy.

Because of the recognized links between family and criminal law, it is also important to be mindful of the need to co-ordinate between different parts of the justice system. The existence of a contact prohibition order in a family law case, for example, would most likely prevent an ADR approach. Other factors like past behaviour and the existence of further criminal charges might require changes to family mediation processes, to ensure both safety and comfort levels of the parties (Madsen). In cases involving child protection mediation, it is especially important for advocates and officials to collaborate, especially where there may be criminal or other legal proceedings (DOJ). In family law ADR matters involving children, there may also be special rules or practices designed to ensure the security of the parties and the effectiveness of the process (AFCC).

PRACTICAL GUIDANCE

Some legal professionals continue to have obligations to their clients engaged in ADR processes based on their traditional roles as advocates. That is, while a procedure like mediation may be more informal and less adversarial, lawyers and paralegals have a duty of loyalty and commitment to their clients. This includes advising them about the risks and benefits of diversions and being competent in respect of the substantive law applicable to their matters, as well as providing guidance about other alternative procedures.

As the criminal court remains the primary forum where people enforce and defend their fundamental rights, it is especially important for defence lawyers to make clear to accuseds that they are entitled to the presumption of innocence and the right to a trial prior to conviction. Legal professionals should have the competency to advise about the risks and benefits of diversions and other alternative proceedings like mediation. Advocates should also be equipped to help manage both diversions and ADR procedures for their clients, as well as formal legal processes. For instance, if a client is interested in mediation, the lawyer can assist them in locating and contracting for the services of a mediator. Depending upon the client's views and preferences, a lawyer may accompany their client to support them through the mediation itself. They will also be tasked with advising on the legality of any memorandum of agreement concluded in a mediation, and may be tasked with helping frame an agreement into a contract or Court Order.

While legal advocates continue to perform their main advocacy functions in criminal law ADR, they do so in different ways, and in a different context. Alternatives to prosecution and ADR like mediation are generally non-adversarial, where parties are encouraged to take a problem-solving approach to resolution. Consequently, some mediators and clients may prefer their own lawyers not to attend or actively participate in the dialogue process resolving criminal disputes through mediation. Depending on the circumstances, some lawyers will simply consult with their clients before or after the mediation in lieu of attending it.

In other cases, however, the need to defend the fundamental substantive and procedural rights of a client may mean that an accused cannot effectively participate in diversions or in criminal ADR without their lawyer present. In either case, given the increasing trend towards the resolution of all disputes outside the courtroom, the use of ADR or diversion in criminal law is likely to continue. Whether through negotiation, diversion, victim-offender mediation, or family law mediation and arbitration, all legal services professionals need to have some familiarity with the important alternatives to formal litigation that are now a vital part of Canada's criminal justice system.

SUMMARY

This chapter has examined ADR in criminal law and other alternatives to prosecution. We began by briefly defining ADR and explaining its place in a justice system that has increasingly sought out alternatives to formal litigation. As in other areas, diversionary procedures like mediation have become an important part of criminal law in Canada. We examined some of the broader alternatives to prosecution, focusing on examples in criminal youth justice and related to the issue of capacity and addressing the challenge of mentally ill accused persons. We then focused in on ADR, to describe the example of victim-offender mediation, setting out its major features, and illustrating its application in the context of a case study involving a recent Canadian criminal matter. We also examined some of the distinct challenges that arise in the use of mediation and arbitration in family law matters that may involve allegations of criminal violence or abuse. Last, the final section overviewed some general practical guidance, and emphasized the need for all legal services practitioners in criminal law to have knowledge and ability with respect to facilitating both diversions and ADR for clients. Our next chapter delves into a further aspect of alternative resolutions, discussing restorative justice, and how it is being implemented in Canada today.

SUGGESTIONS FOR FURTHER READING

Cheng, Helen H.L. "Beyond Forms, Functions and Limits: The Interactionalism of Lon L. Fuller and Its Implications for Alternative Dispute Resolution." (2013) 26 *Can J L & Juris* 2.

Dodek, Adam M. "Canadian Legal Ethics: Ready for the Twenty-First Century at Last." (2008) 46 *Osgoode Hall L J* 1.

Fuller, Lon L. "Collective Bargaining and the Arbitrator." (1963) *Wisc L Rev* 3.

Fuller, Lon L. "Mediation—Its Forms and Functions." (1971) 44 *S Cal L Rev* 305.

Menkel-Meadow, Carrie. "Mothers and Fathers of Invention: The Intellectual Founders of ADR." (2000) 16 *Ohio St Disp Resol* 1.

Shapiro, Martin. *Courts: A Comparative and Political Analysis.* Chicago: University of Chicago Press, 1981.

Wright, M., and B. Galaway, editors. *Mediation and Criminal Justice.* London: Sage, 1989.

ENDNOTES

1.   Though ADR appears as "new," it probably has longstanding and shared roots with formal court procedures. See Shapiro, at 5, where early prototypes for independent courts are said to be based on two disputing parties who "turn to a neutral third party to determine a resolution of the social conflict," much as now occurs with modern mediation and arbitration processes.

2.   Some have argued this may challenge basic notions of transparency and "publicity" in the court system, and note a concerning and decades-long trend of declining court proceedings resulting from privatization, devolution, and outsourcing of litigation, through different means, but including ADR; see Resnik and Curtis, *Representing Justice*, 306–337.

3.   See Lon Fuller's additional articles addressing mediation and arbitration.

4.   Infra.

5.   *Crown Prosecution Manual*, 26 (a). <https://www.ontario.ca/document/crown-prosecution-manual/26-a-mentally-ill-accused-alternatives-prosecution>.

6.   LCO at 5. The presumption of capacity is also codified in various statutes, like, in Ontario, the *Mental Health Act* RSO 1999, c. M.7, and *Substitute Decisions Act*, 1992, SO 1992, c. 30.

7.   Supra note 4.

8.   The 2013 mediation was over compensation for an uncompleted contract and the perpetrator later killed himself; see Neil, "Fatal Shooting." Family law, which often presents emotionally charged issues with vulnerable parties, may present even greater risks of threats, violence, and the potential for abuse.

9.   At s 8 of the province's *Family Law Act*.

10.   See "Annex 4: Family Violence Responses by Jurisdiction" in DOJ.

REFERENCES

Arbitration Act, 1991, SO 1991, c. 17.

Association of Family and Conciliation Courts (AFCC). "Guidelines for Child Protection Mediation." 2012. <https://www.afccnet.org/Portals/0/Guidelines%20for%20Child%20Protection%20Mediation.pdf>. Accessed March 12, 2019.

Bromwich, Rebecca, and Thomas Harrison. "Protecting the Public in
the Twilight of Trials: Ways Forward Towards Access to Justice in
Relational Conflict via the Regulation of Mediator," in Rebecca
Bromwich, Olivia Ungar, and Noémie Richard, editors, *Critical
Perspectives on 21st Century Friendship: Polyamory, Polygamy, and Platonic
Affinity*. Toronto: Demeter Press, 2019.

Bush, Robert A. Baruch, and Joseph Folger. *The Promise of Mediation:
Responding to Conflict through Empowerment and Recognition*. San
Francisco: Jossey-Bass, 1994.

Canadian Community Justice Initiatives Association (CCJIA). <http://
www.cjibc.org/vomp_stories>.

Criminal Code of Canada RSC 1985, c, C-46 [*Criminal Code*].

Department of Justice (Canada; DOJ). "Out-of-Court Dispute Resolution,"
in *Making the Links in Family Violence Cases: Collaboration among the
Family, Child Protection and Criminal Justice Systems*. Report of the
Federal-Provincial Territorial (FPT) Ad Hoc Working Group on Family
Violence, November 2013. <https://www.justice.gc.ca/eng/rp-pr/cj-jp/
fv-vf/mlfvc-elcvf/mlfvc-elcvf.pdf>.

Emond, D. Paul. "Introduction: The Practices of Alternative Dispute
Resolution." (1998) 36:4 *Osgoode Hall L J* 617–623.

Engel, Beverly. "The Power of Apology: How to Give and Receive an
Apology. And It's Worth It, on Both Ends." (2002) *Psychology Today*.
<https://www.psychologytoday.com/ca/articles/200207/the-power-
apology>. Accessed March 16, 2019.

Family Law Act, RSO 1990, c F.3.

Federation of Law Societies. *Model Code of Professional Conduct* [FLSC,
Model Code], as amended March 14, 2017. <https://flsc.ca/wp-content/
uploads/2018/03/Model-Code-as-amended-March-2017-Final.pdf>.
Accessed January 20, 2019.

Fuller, Lon L. "The Forms and Limits of Adjudication." (1978) 92 *Harv L
Rev* 353.

Law Commission of Ontario (LCO). *Legal Capacity, Decision-Making and
Guardianship*. Discussion Paper, 2017. <https://www.lco-cdo.org/en/
our-current-projects/legal-capacity-decision-making-and-guardianship/
legal-capacity-decision-making-and-guardianship-discussion-paper-2/>.
Accessed March 15, 2019.

Linton, Hillary. "Risky Business: Why Family Mediator-Arbitrators Should Take Risk Screening Seriously." (2014) *Canadian Arbitration and Mediation Journal* 59–62.

Luban, David. "The Adversary System Excuse," in *Legal Ethics and Human Dignity*. Cambridge: Cambridge University Press, 2007.

MacFarlane, Julie. *Dispute Resolution Readings and Case Studies*, 3rd ed. Toronto: Emond Montgomery Publications, 2011.

Madsen, Lene. "A Fine Balance: Domestic Violence, Screening and Family Mediation." (2012) 30:3 *Can Fam LQ* 343.

Mental Health Act, RSO 1999, c M.7.

Ministry of the Attorney General—Ontario Criminal Law Division. *Crown Prosecution Manual.* <https://www.ontario.ca/document/crown-prosecution-manual>. Accessed March 9, 2019 [*Crown Prosecution Manual*].

Neil, Martha. "Fatal Shooting after Mediation Leaves Lawyer and Client Dead." *ABA Journal*, 2013, January 31. <http://www.abajournal.com/news/article/lawyer_shot_client_executive_killed_after_mediation_session_with_suspected_/>. Accessed March 12, 2019.

Ontario Association for Family Mediation (OAFM). "Policy on Intimate Partner Violence and Power Imbalances." 2013. <https://www.oafm.on.ca/about/standards/policy-on-intimate-partner-violence-and-power-imbalances/>. Accessed March 10, 2019.

Resnik, Judith, and Dennis Curtis. *Representing Justice*. New Haven, CT: Yale University Press, 2011.

Rosenberg, Marc. "The Attorney General and the Prosecution Function in the Twenty-First Century." (2009) 43:2 *Queen's LJ* 813.

Shapiro, Martin. "The Prototype of Courts," in *Courts: A Comparative and Political Analysis*. Chicago: University of Chicago Press, 1981.

Substitute Decisions Act, 1992, SO 1992, c 30.

Umbreit, M. S. "Mediation of Victim Offender Conflict." (1988) 84 *Journ Disp Res* [Umbreit, "Mediation"].

Umbreit, M. S. *The Handbook of Victim-Offender Mediation*. San Francisco: Jossey-Bass, 2001 [Umbreit, *Handbook*].

Wainwright v Wainwright, (2012) ONSC 2868 CanLII [*Wainwright*].

Youth Criminal Justice Act, SC 2002, c 1 [YCJA].

CHAPTER 5

Restorative Justice: Theory, Practice, Standards, and Guidance

LEARNING OBJECTIVES

After reading this chapter, students should better understand:

- The concept of restorative justice, principles, and definition issues
- Restorative justice practices
- Restorative approaches in criminal and youth justice systems in Canada
- Standards for restorative procedures for lawyers and legal system professionals
- Practical guidance and best practices for implementing restorative justice

OVERVIEW

This chapter builds and expands on the discussion of ADR procedures in criminal justice begun in Chapter 4. As noted there, victim-offender mediation is one mechanism through which restorative justice approaches are implemented. This chapter turns its focus to the larger conceptual framework, to look at restorative approaches more generally, along with some of the legislation, policy, practices, and procedures that fall within this label.

This chapter starts by providing a working definition of restorative justice. It goes on to outline the key practices that have been considered restorative in the legal system. Subsequently, we look at how the concept of restorative justice is now incorporated into Canada's criminal justice system. We discuss specific restorative approaches, including a case study to illustrate how this alternative resolution approach is used in Canadian criminal law practices. Building on this case study, we then identify the standards of restorative justice, and provide some professional guidance to legal services professionals in general, and to lawyers specifically, who may work in this area.

UNDERSTANDING RESTORATIVE JUSTICE

The term *restorative justice* was first introduced and became widespread in criminal justice literature over 40 years ago, building on the work of leading scholars in the field (Zehr). Some commentators claim the term was first coined in the late 1970s (Van Ness and Strong; Eglash), but there is evidence to suggest that the roots of restorative justice are much more ancient, reaching back into traditional social customs (Braithwaite, *Responsive Regulation*; Gavrielides, "Restorative Practices"). Others claim that restorative justice principles may be grounded in traditions of justice as old as ancient Greek and Roman civilizations (Gavrielides, *Handbook*).

Typically, restorative approaches to justice are distinguished from the historical emphasis in the legal system, that people "should pay for their criminal acts," as a kind of "retribution." Howard Zehr's definition of these two terms illustrates the contrast between these two approaches. On the one hand, traditional **retributive justice** approaches regard "crime as a violation of the state, defined by lawbreaking and guilt. Justice determines blame and administers pain in a contest between offender and the state directed by systematic rules." On the other hand, **restorative justice** perspectives see "crime as a violation of people and relationships. It creates obligations to make things right. Justice involves the victim, the offender, and the community in search for solutions which promote repair, reconciliation, and reassurance" (Zehr, *Restorative Justice for Our Times*, 183).

One more recent definition presents restorative justice as "an ethos with practical goals." From this perspective, the goals of restorative justice include addressing harm by directly or indirectly including affected parties in the resolution process, which also includes voluntary and honest dialogue to achieve understanding (Gavrielides, *Theory & Practice*, 139). In this way, restorative justice adopts a less adversarial and less strictly retributive approach to conflicts and their control, retaining at the same time some rehabilitative objectives (Gavrielides, *Theory & Practice*, 139). Nowadays, it is widely accepted that use of the term *restorative justice* in the justice system can refer to at least four different circumstances, the first of which is victim-offender mediation, discussed in Chapter 4. Restorative justice approaches have also been used in family group conferences; healing and sentencing circles; and Community Restorative Boards (Gavrielides, *Theory & Practice*, "Restorative Justice").

To be considered "restorative" in the broader sense, programs implementing this approach need to include the offender, the victim, and the representatives of their communities. It is also essential that these practices maintain and express restorative justice's neutrality on the matter of whose interests should come first in the justice process. This is because according to generally accepted understandings of restorative justice, it does not prefer the interests of any of the parties involved in a case. From this viewpoint, both victims and offenders are equally important to restore harm. Consequently, their equal treatment and voluntary participation is needed throughout the process.

There is general consensus that modern approaches to restorative justice were developed in response to criticisms of the traditional criminal justice system. These critiques saw the overall legal system as too formalistic, punitive, and adversarial. In this way, criminal law may fail to serve the wider needs of victims, as well as the interests of offenders.

The first modern restorative program is widely viewed as having been developed in Canada in 1974. Two youths from Elmira, Ontario, went on a drunken rampage, vandalizing multiple properties, causing thousands of dollars of damage in their community. Working with the court, local parole and court workers developed an alternative to penal sanctions, where the young offenders instead visited the 22 homes of their victims and negotiated reparations with each. This alternative sentence is regarded as one of the first reconciliation programs to formally implement restorative justice principles in court in the world (Zehr, *Restorative Justice for Our Times*, 159–161). The restorative approach used in this Ontario incident has since been modelled in more than 50 countries, and is the subject of a recent documentary film (CJI).

Restorative justice can be contrasted to retributive justifications of the criminal justice system. In this sense, the main goal of criminal law has traditionally been narrowly focused on discerning blame and assessing guilt. Restorative justice principles and practices seek to allow space that includes a greater role for victims to determine the outcomes in cases. As in the Elmira case, rather than excluding offenders from their communities where harm has taken place, this approach seeks to include them to address the damage caused to the victim by criminal behaviour, but also potentially to other community members as well. In this respect, one of the main features of restorative justice is to enable a place where affected individuals can engage in face-to-face encounters to "tell their truths" (Llewellyn and Howse).

The character of these direct restorative encounters can vary in form. One, discussed in the last chapter, is through mediation between the victim and offender. Other forms consist of community circles, or of more focused conferences. As Braithwaite describes, restorative justice is

> a process where all stakeholders affected by an injustice have an opportunity to discuss how they have been affected by the injustice and to decide what should be done to repair the harm. With crime, restorative justice is about the idea that because crime hurts, justice should heal. It follows that conversations with those who have been hurt and with those who have inflicted the harm must be central to the process. (Braithwaite, "De-Professionalization")

Restorative justice is premised in part on a theory of human behaviour that regards it as depending on relations; in principle, this approach to resolving criminal harm addresses the personal and social connections among community members, offenders, and society as a whole.

As suggested above, and despite its recent implementation in the modern court system, notions of restorative justice are infused with many ancient and Indigenous traditions. This includes practices from the Indigenous peoples in Canada as well as others, for example from the Maori of New Zealand. Over the past 40 years, Canada's criminal justice system has incorporated restorative justice principles and practices in a growing variety of ways either pre- or post-sentence, in prison, or as a preventative practice in the community (Gavrielides, "Restorative Justice").

For example, on sentence, the obligation to consider Indigenous heritage is codified in s 718.2(e) of the *Criminal Code*. As we noted in Chapter 3, Canada's Indigenous peoples are vastly over-represented in prisons, so one goal of this provision is to seek out meaningful and culturally appropriate alternatives to jail (*Gladue*). In a 2012 decision, the Supreme Court also reminded trial judges "to the extent that current sentencing practices do not further these objectives, those practices must change so as to meet the needs of Aboriginal offenders and their communities" (*Ipeelee*, para 66–67).

At least 14 specialized "Indigenous Peoples' Courts" have been established in Ontario, British Columbia, Alberta, and Saskatchewan (Advocates' Society, 65). Whether a special forum exists in any given jurisdiction or not, it's important to determine at an early stage if a client identifies as Indigenous (*Kreko*), since this may be an important factor in how a court deals with a matter. Determining indigeneity may be fraught by the reluctance of some individuals to identify with First Nations because of negative past experiences or difficulties in establishing heritage (Advocates' Society). However, the obligation is shared across the country, between both Crown and defence, to adduce evidence where Indigenous heritage may be a factor (*Wells*; *Kakekagamick*).

Judges who preside over these hearings incorporate traditional approaches to sentencing, such as healing and sentencing circles, and community council programs. While the effects of restorative justice are perhaps most prominent on sentence, restorative principles and indigeneity may also be considered at various stages of criminal processes, including bail (*Gladue*), jury selection, and, following sentence, in determining parole (*Twins*, ss 80–84). Importantly, these considerations are not about an offender's "Indigenousness" amounting to a "mitigation" as a factor in determining these issues (Advocates' Society, 68), but about finding a different approach to addressing the adverse effects of criminality to meet the wide-ranging needs of the community.

VICTIM-OFFENDER MEDIATION

In Chapter 4, we discussed victim-offender mediation as one of the alternative procedures available in criminal law. From its earliest roots in the Elmira case and from a broader perspective, this type of mediation is one of the most well-known and commonly used contemporary restorative programs in Europe and the US. In its typical form, it brings together the primary victim and offender using a trained mediator to co-ordinate the meeting. When both parties have had their say, the mediator helps them consider ways to make things right.

As part of a restorative justice approach, victim-mediation programs can also appear in various shapes and forms. The character of these programs also varies across jurisdictions, based on things like the level of tolerance coming from the public, the political agendas, as well as the cultural and historical background of the country. Building on our description of mediation between victims and offenders in Canadian law set out in Chapter 4, these procedural variables situate Canadian practices in a larger comparative perspective.

Various kinds of mediation programs utilize restorative frameworks in different places and can be classified into two broad categories. The first category distinguishes three different types of mediation schemes based on their relation with traditional criminal justice systems: "independent," "relatively independent," and "dependent." Programs are independent when they are offered as real alternatives for criminal litigation, diverting the criminal case out of the formal process. This occurs at a very early stage of the case, replacing any penal response to crime. An example is the Dutch process of *dading*, which involves negotiating a settlement between the parties. The final outcome precludes re-entrance of the case in the criminal justice system.

Other procedures can be relatively independent when offered as part of regular criminal procedures. This can take place at any stage when a case is diverted and referred to a mediator, whose task is to reach an agreement between victim and offender. If successful, this agreement can have an impact on the outcome of the criminal proceedings, often involving a reduction in the formal sentence. Finally, mediation projects can be dependent when they are situated adjacent to the conventional system. This model is used after the criminal trial has run its course, and is mainly employed in instances of the most serious crime or in the prison context.

The second category of victim-mediation programs can be distinguished in a number of potentially overlapping ways. The first is between programs that are primarily oriented towards the needs of the offender, and those that also take account of the needs of the victim. The second distinction is made between projects where victims meet their offenders and projects where groups of victims take part in discussions with unrelated offenders. Although this latter type of mediation does not preclude bringing the individuals together to consider how offenders can make amends, their main goal is to help both victims and offenders challenge each other's prejudices.

Third, some mediation programs may include face-to-face meetings between victim and offender, and have mediators act only as go-betweens. The fourth distinction depends on the cases that the mediation programs accept. For instance, a project may take cases below or above a certain level of seriousness, or only juvenile cases. Lastly, there are victim-mediation programs carried out by paid professional staff or by trained volunteers.

To sum up, overall victim-offender mediation can appear as part of, instead of, or on top of the structure of the formal criminal justice system. As the appreciation of alternative and restorative practices continues to grow, aspects of these different approaches may appear or be appropriate for implementation in the Canadian context.

In general, the process of all types of programs follows the same basic phases, which we described in Chapter 4 and in further detail here. The first step is a referral of the case to the mediation program. Referrals usually come from the system's agents (such as police, prosecutors, judges, and probation officers), and may take place at any time from the report of

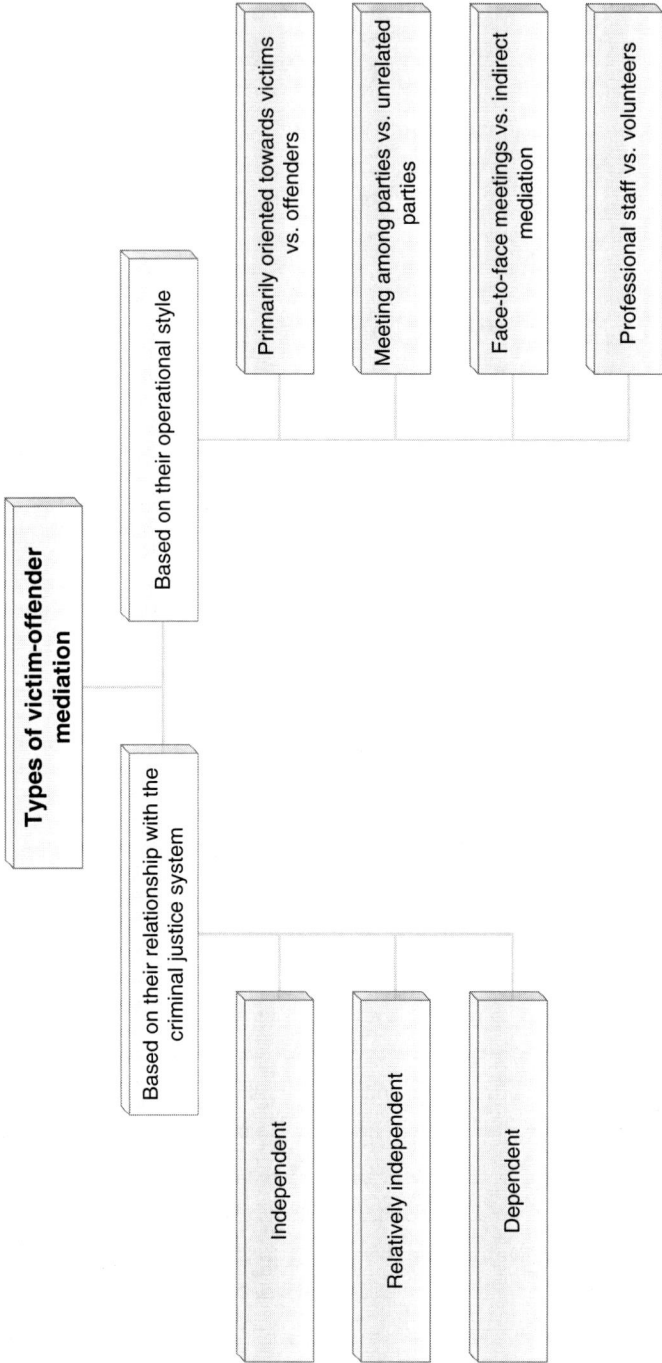

Figure 1: Classification of Victim-Offender Mediation Programs

Source: Created by Theo Gavrielides (2007).

the crime to the parole period. The second step is the preparation of the case. Victim and offender are contacted separately, and asked if they are interested in joining the mediation program. The facilitator then gathers information about the offence, and schedules the session.

The third step is the actual meeting between the offender and the victim. Here, the structure of the meeting varies accordingly, and depends in part on special contextual concerns that may raise issues, like the nature of the crime, the type of proceedings, and other factors like the age and capacity of the individuals involved, who might also be subject to distinct procedures, based on things like indigeneity. The final step involves preparing the file and returning it to the referral source.

FAMILY GROUP CONFERENCING (RESTORATIVE CONFERENCING)

One important consideration that may affect restorative approaches is the type of legal proceeding. In Chapter 4, we discussed mediation and arbitration in family law. In that area, we highlighted the special risks of engaging in alternative approaches where criminal violence or abuse may be an issue in family or child protection proceedings. From the larger restorative justice perspective, Family Group Conferencing, or restorative conferencing, is another variation of restorative justice that is also a widely utilized practice in Canadian criminal law more generally.

We should note that the Family Group Conferencing can been used for either private or public law disputes, though our focus in this work lends itself to further consideration of the latter context. When implemented for criminal cases, group conferencing involves more parties as compared to standard criminal mediations involving victims and offenders (Doak and O'Mahony). In particular, not only are primary victims and offenders included, but also sometimes secondary victims, the parties' families, close friends, community representatives, or the police.[1] All these people are welcomed, because they are connected to at least one of the primary participants. They are brought together by an impartial third party, who is usually trained for this task and facilitates the interactions, though they do not play a role in the substantive discussion.

Family Group Conferences can be "unscripted" or "scripted." Scripted conferences occur when the facilitator follows a prescribed pattern in guiding discussion. As with victim-offender mediation more generally, a necessary pre-condition to this restorative approach is that the offender has admitted to the crime and that all parties are participating out of their own will and desire to reconcile and restore their relationship in a sincere and humane way. Typically, the process starts with offenders' descriptions of what happened, and whom they think are affected by their actions. Victims then describe their experience and the harmful effects it has had on their lives. Offenders are directly faced with the human impact the incident had on their victims and their family, and, of course, on their own family and friends. However, restored relationships and feelings are not the only possible outcomes of this program.

Together, the group decides what the offender needs to do to repair the harm, and what assistance the offender will need in doing so. Victims are asked what "practical outcomes" they expect from the conference, in order to shape the appropriate obligations for the offender. The session ends with parties signing an agreement outlining their expectations and commitments to each other. All participants may take part in carrying out the final agreement, which is then sent to the appropriate officials.

Family Group Conferencing can be used in multiple stages of the criminal process. Most often however, it is used by police as an alternative to arrest and referral to the formal criminal justice system. This has led to a unique linkage between restorative justice and the formal justice system. Overall, this program provides the victim, the offender, and all those affected a chance to contribute to a discussion intended to formulate sanctions and amends. The chance for those directly impacted to narrate "their story" increases offender awareness of the human impact of their actions, and provides an opportunity for those convicted to regret, apologize, take full responsibility, and be forgiven by their victim and community. In this way, it may shape their future behaviour, relying on local social and inherent support systems to address the issue and restore relations within the community.

HEALING AND SENTENCING/PEACEKEEPING AND PEACEMAKING CIRCLES

Circles are community-directed processes, usually working side-by-side with the criminal justice system. They originate from traditional circle rituals, where Indigenous peoples[2] gathered to discuss their conflicts and find solutions, and are commonly found in both Canada and Australia. Today, they typically involve a multi-step procedure, which starts with an application by offenders to participate in the process, and continues with a "healing circle" for them and their victims (Walker and Davidson). If the discussion in the healing circle proves to be constructive, helpful, and sincere, then a "sentencing circle" is formed for the discussion on the elements of a sentencing plan. After all parties have agreed to a sentence, "follow-up circles" at various intervals may be formed to monitor the progress of the offender.

Circles are similar to the Family Group Conferencing described in the previous section in that they expand participation beyond the primary victim and offender. However, in this case, any additional member of the community who has an interest in the case may participate. These can be: the victim, the offender, their families and friends, judges, as well as court personnel, prosecutors, defence counsel, and police.

All participants sit in a circle, and the process typically begins with an explanation of what happened. Subsequently, everyone is given the opportunity to talk. The discussion moves from person to person around the circle using a "talking piece," with anyone saying whatever they wish and continues until everything that needs to be said has been said. There is a "keeper of the circle," whose role is to ensure that the process is protected.

The overall goal is to promote healing for all injured parties, and an opportunity for the offender to make amends to the victim and to the society. This program promotes a sense of community, empowering its participants by giving them a voice and a shared responsibility in a process whereby all parties try to find constructive solutions. Circles are used at various stages both within and outside the criminal process.

COMMUNITY RESTORATIVE BOARDS

Community Restorative (or Reparative) Boards (CRBs) are a typical example of community members becoming substantially involved in the justice process. CRBs are small groups of active citizens, specifically trained to conduct public, face-to-face meetings with offenders "sentenced" by the court to participate. CRBs provide an opportunity for victims and the community to confront offenders in a constructive manner, while giving the chance to the offender to take personal responsibility. CRBs promote citizens' ownership of the criminal justice system, as they provide them with an opportunity to get directly involved in the justice process, generating meaningful, "community-driven" consequences for criminal actions that are said to reduce costly reliance on formal criminal justice processing.

The process usually involves a meeting with the board members discussing the nature of the offence, and the negative effects it had on the victim and community. After a thorough examination, the board develops a set of proposed sanctions, which they discuss with the offender and the victim, until they all reach an understandable and acceptable agreement. Then, they talk about the method, specific actions, and timetable for the reparation of the crime. Subsequently, offenders have to document their progress in fulfilling the exact terms of the agreement. The process ends when the stipulated period of time has elapsed, and the board has submitted a report to the court on the offender's compliance with the agreed-upon sanctions.

RESTORATIVE JUSTICE IN CRIMINAL AND YOUTH JUSTICE SYSTEMS

For over 40 years, engaged citizens and NGOs have worked both independently and together in a movement to establish restorative justice in Canada. They have had significant success, at least to the extent that this movement has influenced how we *talk* about the administration of criminal justice. In 1988, the Canadian Parliamentary Standing Committee on Justice and Solicitor General conducted a review of sentencing, conditional release, and related aspects of corrections. In particular, the report recommended that the government "supports the expansion and evaluation throughout Canada of victim-offender reconciliation programmes at all stages of criminal justice process which: (a) provide substantial support to victims through effective victim services [and] (b) encourage a high degree of community participation" (House of Commons).

This early report also advised that the purposes of sentencing should be enacted in legislation. These purposes include reparation of harm to the victim and the community and promoting a sense of responsibility in offenders. In 1996, these changes were introduced in the *Criminal Code of Canada* (*Criminal Code*, s 718). In the same year, Canada's federal, provincial, and territorial ministers responsible for justice endorsed a report that was written to address the growth in the prison population at that time (Solicitor General). One of the recommendations was to increase the use of restorative justice and share information on the results of demonstration projects based on its principles.

After a 1997 conference on restorative justice sponsored by the Canadian Criminal Justice Association and the International Centre for Criminal Law Reform and Criminal Justice Policy, a working group composed of senior officials from federal, provincial, and territorial governments was established. Its mandate was to collaborate in elaboration of policies for restorative justice, and promote and disseminate research and share information on developments in the various Canadian jurisdictions.

In subsequent 1997, 1998, and 2000 reports by the Solicitor General, most Canadian jurisdictions reported the introduction of restorative policies and programs. In 2000, the Department of Justice prepared a consultation paper titled *Restorative Justice in Canada*, with an overview of the nature of restorative justice and its application in Canada. The consultation questions included in the paper aimed to address:

(a)   the role of Government and community in restorative approaches;

(b)   the effects of victims, appropriate offences for restorative process;

(c)   accountability issues; and

(d)   training and standards of practice (DOJ).

Since that time, alternatives to traditional criminal justice procedures that incorporate restorative practices and perspectives have continued to flourish. In 2015, Canada's Parliament passed the Canadian *Victims' Bill of Rights*. The *Bill of Rights* expressly acknowledges and bolsters the rights of victims to have information about criminal proceedings, and to participate in those proceedings. It provides victims statutory rights to information, participation, protection, and restitution, giving new effect to restorative justice principles under Canadian criminal law. That same year, the *Report of the Truth and Reconciliation Commission* on residential schools in Canada made numerous recommendations for changes to the criminal justice system, as well as law and legal education, to redress harms caused by residential schools in Canada.

The importance of the above legislative amendments is also reflected in jurisprudence from the Supreme Court of Canada (*Gladue*). The Court has rejected the view that a restorative approach is more lenient in dealing with crime, or that a sentence focussing on restorative justice is a lighter sentence. In particular, the Court determined that restoring harmony involves determining sentences that respond to the needs of the victim, the community, and the offender (*Proulx*, paras 16–20). The Court also pointed out that practice should now be directed towards alternative ends, including less reliance on incarceration as a sanction, and the increased use of restorative principles in sentencing.

In Canada, restorative justice practices have been implemented in relation to minor criminal offending, especially by youths. As early as 1998, the Government of Canada developed a Youth Justice Strategy, which eventually resulted in the *Youth Criminal Justice Act* (YCJA). This was passed by Parliament in 2002, becoming effective on April 1, 2003. As we noted in Chapter 4, important alternatives within that legislation include provision for "extrajudicial measures," as well as "extrajudicial sanctions" made within the discretion of the Crown (YCJA, s 9).

Changes to the youth justice regime in Canada have also been the subject of some critical scrutiny. For example, in his analysis for the 6th International Conference on Restorative Justice, one commentator said:

> We cannot escape the conclusion that the YCJA draws upon a hodge-podge of perspectives from a social reaction point of view. While

several of its principles reflect a restorative perspective, its structure is undeniably penal in nature. The terms used in this legislation refer to sentences, and one of its very significant provisions would have young offenders found guilty of a serious offence subject to adult sentences, thereby endorsing the notion that harsh sentences are effective. Several of the stated principles and objectives are inspired by the rehabilitative model, thus limiting the restorative approach to less serious offences. Beyond its stated objectives, the YCJA identifies the police as first interveners and gives them the discretion to apply a series of non-judicial measures in the case of minor offences. As a result, the mission of the police and the professional ideology of police officers take on added importance. (Charbonneau, 8)

The implementation of restorative justice in Canada has also raised other concerns. For example, a 1998 report from the Standing Committee on Justice and Human Rights expressed fears that restorative programs might end up being used inappropriately, failing to denounce and deter serious crime. Robert Cormier, Deputy Director General in the Department of the Solicitor General, was concerned that "RJ programmes are dominated by NGOs with a primary mandate to assist offenders in their rehabilitations and reintegration, and that the perspective of victims has not been adequately taken into account in the design and implementation of these programmes" (Cormier).

The new emphasis on restorative justice also raised issues amongst practitioners, who worried about the absence of guidelines, especially in relation to victim participation, power imbalances, serious crimes, and the training of facilitators. Victim groups also seemed to be nervous of losing funding for services already offered by the mainstream system to victims. For example, the head of one victims' rights organization said: "To my knowledge [RJ] programmes [in Canada] are set up with very little or no victim input. They are being implemented so fast that not enough skilled facilitators can be found. The resulting scenario is one of well-meaning but naïve volunteers operating in poorly-run programs and a likelihood of the re-victimisation[;] ... the RJ agenda benefits the offender more than the victim" (Simmonds). Concerns were also reported that while restorative justice practice may encourage offenders' participation, their rights may also end up being compromised (Brown).

Finally, many have argued the restorative justice process can undermine other sentencing principles. One evaluation of the effectiveness of victim-offender mediation, for example, suggested that the restorative focus on repairing harm in an individualized manner often put in danger the "proportionality" principle. Proportionality in criminal law refers to the idea that the severity of punishment should reflect the seriousness of the crime (Roberts). However, the public's expectation, probably based on their familiarity with the retributive goals of the criminal justice system, may lead them to reject sentences with restorative aims, which could be perceived as not sufficiently punitive in serious crimes.

Despite criticisms, there are now restorative justice programs in place across the country. In many Canadian regions, restorative justice programs are variable in terms of their delivery model and accessibility, depending upon the not-for-profit services that provide them, as well as the inclinations of particular jurisdictional governments. For instance, Nova Scotia has taken a leading role in this area. As of 2016, it had established a province-wide Restorative Justice Program for adults as well as youths. There have also been an increasing number of attempts to address Indigenous offending through culturally sensitive restorative processes (Cawsey).

More recently, there has also been a trend in Canadian jurisdictions to expand the application of restorative justice principles and practices to a broader range of offences. This expansion of restorative justice practices has sometimes included extension of restorative techniques to complex cases, such as white-collar or corporate crimes. A current example in Canadian law is the passage of legislation in 2018 to amend the *Criminal Code* to allow for "Remediation Agreements" (s 715.3), sometimes also known as "Deferred Prosecution Agreements," or DPAs. These agreements are intended to hold organizations accountable for white-collar crime through denunciation, penalties, by imposing corrective measures, providing reparations, and seeking to reduce the harm of corporate misconduct on individuals (*Criminal Code*, s 715.31).

Though new to Canadian law, these kinds of extensions of restorative justice are common in other countries (Anand). Recent expansions of restorative principles reflect the ongoing adaptation of the traditional justice system to incorporate this alternative perspective, which got its first start in the court system in the Canadian town of Elmira in the 1970s.

CASE STUDY: Restorative Justice

The following case study is adapted from the Restorative Justice website of the Province of Nova Scotia (https://novascotia.ca/just/RJ/):

One night, two intoxicated young adults went exploring through a building on university property. While inside, they took a very expensive piece of equipment from a classroom. During the theft, the stolen item was damaged. The next morning when the instructors entered their classroom, they discovered the equipment was missing and they were devastated. Without this equipment students wouldn't be able to complete their required assignments for the year.

Because, in November 2016, the Nova Scotia Restorative Justice Program was expanded and adults were given the option to participate in the program, this matter was referred by the Crown. The Restorative Justice Program provides an opportunity for those who have caused harm, those who have been affected, and those who can support the participants to come together to talk about what happened, share the impacts, and work on a plan together to repair the harm. The university identified representatives from the school who would attend the restorative meeting to share the impact this offence had on the school and community. They wanted their voice to be heard and to have input into what would help them move forward.

Both adults accepted responsibility for their role in the offence; they were remorseful and ashamed of their behaviour. Once the restorative process was underway both started to think about the impact their actions had on the school, the students, and the community. They could see that their actions had a ripple effect.

At the restorative meeting, representatives from the university were able to explain how this piece of equipment was an integral part of their program, how hundreds of students were affected

Continued

by their actions, and how both staff and students shared an un-necessary financial burden. The university had the opportunity to hear the individuals accept responsibility and express their remorse.

Through both the university program and the Restorative Justice Program these two young adults were able to arrange paying resti-tution for the equipment, apologize for their actions, and work with campus security to get a better understanding of the valuable work they do to keep the campus safe.

All parties were satisfied with the process and felt their voices were heard.

Case Study Discussion

1. What specific facts made the restorative justice program effective in this case?
2. What about the case overall made it a good context for the use of restorative justice?
3. Are there some ways in which a restorative justice approach, like that implemented in the case study, might not be welcomed by poli-ticians, victims' groups, or the general public? Why?

Traditional purposes of criminal sentencing include retribution, but also rehabilitation, restitution, and deterrence. Using this case study as an example, think about the ways that restorative approaches comple-ment or detract from these additional objectives.

PROFESSIONAL STANDARDS AND PRACTICAL GUIDANCE IN RESTORATIVE JUSTICE

Advocacy for clients in alternative approaches like restorative justice requires professional behaviour. Alternatives to the adversarial crim-inal justice system often occur outside the direct scrutiny of a court, but complement its more formal proceedings, and may involve community advocates, including elders, social workers, parole and probation officers, as well as lawyers and paralegals. The widespread introduction of restorative justice across Canada, and around the world, has led to some consideration of the need for common professional standards to steer the implementation of this approach in criminal law. This includes a United Nations statement establishing a common set of "Basic Principles" in restorative justice, included for further reference at the end of this chapter.

Considerations of overall standards to guide restorative procedures and practice (Braithwaite, *Responsive Regulation*) generally fall into three broad categories.

1. Constraining Standards: These aim to specify precise *rights and limits* for restorative justice and are: non-domination; empowerment of all parties; honouring legally specific upper limits on sanctions; respectful listening; equal concern for all stakeholders; accountability; and respect for human rights.

2. Maximizing Standards: These aim to *maximize the impact* of restorative justice and include: restoration of human dignity, property loss, safety, damaged relationships, communities, environment, freedom, compassion, peace, sense of duty as a citizen and emotions; provision of social support; and prevention of future injustice.

3. Emergent Standards: These are *gifts* of restorative justice and should not be demanded but merely welcomed as consequences of a successful process and could include: apology; forgiveness; remorse; mercy; censure of the act.

As a practical matter, there are some specific things individuals and organizations involved in restorative justice should do,[3] based on the principles and standards of restorative justice described above. In addition to the explicit ethical obligations that may be imposed on legal professionals, everyone working in criminal law should advise clients about the risks and benefits of restorative justice.

This also means that lawyers and other justice system professionals should educate themselves about what restorative processes are available in their area, and how these can be accessed. This may be challenging, since restorative justice alternatives are often operated by a network of not-for-profit NGOs, so it is not always obvious what services are available in an area or how they can be accessed. It is helpful that Justice Canada maintains an online directory of restorative justice programs across Canada (see http://www.justice.gc.ca/eng/cj-jp/rj-jr/sch-rch.aspx).

As is the case with other ADR processes discussed in Chapter 4, defence lawyers must not abandon their role in safeguarding the presumption of innocence, or in advising more generally about substantive legal matters. One potential risk in restorative justice mirrors challenges in ensuring that plea bargaining is not used improperly to expedite criminal procedures to the detriment of innocent persons charged with criminal offences, as we described in Chapter 2. It is crucially important that restorative justice is also not improperly used as a means to "net-widen," or sanction accuseds for whom a guilty finding was not a reasonable prospect.

Legal advocates must make clear to accuseds that they are entitled to the presumption of innocence and have the right to a trial. In many cases, professionals tasked with adversarially presenting client interests in the formal criminal justice process do not participate in the restorative justice resolutions. However, depending upon client preferences and the procedures of the agency providing the service, they might be involved directly or indirectly. Lawyers, paralegals, and others who perform more traditional advocacy roles in court should consult both before and after a restorative justice sentencing circle, conference, or other circle process takes place, to ensure their clients' rights are protected.

Where professionals take on roles, such as facilitation or sitting as a participant in a sentencing circle, peacemaking circle, community meeting, youth justice committee, victim-offender meeting, or some other encounter framed as a restorative justice process, they should communicate clearly their role. It must be well-defined to all participants who the professionals represent, or if they are acting as a neutral. Lawyers and criminal justice system professionals are bound by their professional ethics to avoid conflicts of interest, so they cannot both sit as a neutral in a restorative justice process and represent one party unless they have express prior permission from the parties to do so.

CRITICAL COMMENT ON RESTORATIVE JUSTICE

Restorative justice appeals to reformers and policy-makers who want to see a change in focus in the justice system, towards reducing the risk of repeat offenders. This change is probably driven in part by a recognition of the high social and financial cost of the criminal justice system, with an increasing prison population and growing costs for policing, prosecution, and corrections. In addition to addressing costs, restorative justice holds out the potential of a more holistic approach to harm and inclusivity.

For example, the involvement of victims in the restorative process is a welcome change in how criminal justice is delivered. Some have argued that, in a shifting policy and legislative environment where the Canadian federal government is determined to bring a change in how victims are served, they need to be heard directly (Gavrielides, "The Victims' Directive"). Some research suggests that most victims do want to talk and be included in the formation of practices and policies, like restorative justice, that impact on them (Gavrielides, "The Victims' Directive," "London Case Study"). However, there may be continuing questions about whether policy and legislative changes alone can shift the entrenched adversarialism in criminal law, and the traditional retributive mindsets that largely define modern criminal justice. Without these changes, though, the movement to incorporate more restorative practices and approaches into the Canadian criminal justice system will continue to face challenges (Gavrielides, 2018).

SUMMARY

This chapter has looked at restorative justice. We started by exploring how the concept is defined in contrast to the more traditional retributive justice goals of the criminal justice system. We then looked specifically at ways it is incorporated into Canada's legal system, highlighting criminal youth justice. The case study included in the chapter showed a recent practical application of a restorative justice approach in Canadian law, its procedural features, and some potential outcomes.

We also consider some standards of restorative justice as established by the United Nations, and as part of theoretical considerations in managing ethical obligations in this approach. We described some professional implications for lawyers and legal system professionals, building on the identified standards in this section. Last, we presented some practical guidance for legal system professionals involved in restorative justice and concluded with critical reflection to identify current and future challenges in the expanding implementation of restorative approaches in Canada. Our next and final chapter elevates the discussion about conflict resolution to explore the importance of self-care for professionals who work in the legal system and use negotiation and other alternative approaches to resolve criminal disputes.

"Basic principles on the use of restorative justice programmes in criminal matters," ECOSOC Res. 2000/14, U.N. Doc. E/2000/INF/2/Add.2 at 35 (2000)

Annex

Preliminary draft elements of a declaration of basic principles on the use of restorative justice programmes in criminal matters

I. Definitions

1. "Restorative justice programme" means any programme that uses restorative processes or aims to achieve restorative outcomes.

2. "Restorative outcome" means an agreement reached as the result of a restorative process. Examples of restorative outcomes include restitution, community service and any other programme or response designed to accomplish reparation of the victim and community, and reintegration of the victim and/or the offender.

3. "Restorative process" means any process in which the victim, the offender and/or any other individuals or community members affected by a crime actively participate together in the resolution of matters arising from the crime, often with the help of a fair and impartial third party. Examples of restorative process include mediation, conferencing and sentencing circles.

4. "Parties" means the victim, the offender and any other individuals or community members affected by a crime who may be involved in a restorative justice programme.

5. "Facilitator" means a fair and impartial third party whose role is to facilitate the participation of victims and offenders in an encounter programme.

II. Use of restorative justice programmes

6. Restorative justice programmes should be generally available at all stages of the criminal justice process.

7. Restorative processes should be used only with the free and voluntary consent of the parties. The parties should be able to withdraw such consent at any time during the process. Agreements should be arrived at voluntarily by the parties and contain only reasonable and proportionate obligations.

8. All parties should normally acknowledge the basic facts of a case as a basis for participation in a restorative process. Participation should not be used as evidence of admission of guilt in subsequent legal proceedings.

9. Obvious disparities with respect to factors such as power imbalances and the parties' age, maturity or intellectual capacity should be taken into consideration in referring a case to and in conducting a restorative process. Similarly, obvious threats to any of the parties' safety should also be considered in referring any case to and in conducting a restorative process. The views of the parties themselves about the suitability of restorative processes or outcomes should be given great deference in this consideration.

Continued

10. Where restorative processes and/or outcomes are not possible, criminal justice officials should do all they can to encourage the offender to take responsibility vis-à-vis the victim and affected communities, and reintegration of the victim and/or offender into the community.

III. Operation of restorative justice programmes

11. Guidelines and standards should be established, with legislative authority when necessary, that govern the use of restorative justice programmes. Such guidelines and standards should address:

   (a) The conditions for the referral of cases to restorative justice programmes;

   (b) The handling of cases following a restorative process;

   (c) The qualifications, training and assessment of facilitators;

   (d) The administration of restorative justice programmes;

   (e) Standards of competence and ethical rules governing operation of restorative justice programmes.

12. Fundamental procedural safeguards should be applied to restorative justice programmes and in particular to restorative processes:

   (a) The parties should have the right to legal advice before and after the restorative process and, where necessary, to translation and/or interpretation. Minors should, in addition, have the right to parental assistance;

   (b) Before agreeing to participate in restorative processes, the parties should be fully informed of their rights, the nature of the process and the possible consequences of their decision;

   (c) Neither the victim nor the offender should be induced by unfair means to participate in restorative processes or outcomes.

13. Discussions in restorative processes should be confidential and should not be disclosed subsequently, except with the agreement of the parties.

14. Judicial discharges based on agreements arising out of restorative justice programmes should have the same status as judicial decisions or judgements and should preclude prosecution in respect of the same facts (*non bis in idem*).

15. Where no agreement can be made between the parties, the case should be referred back to the criminal justice authorities and a decision as to how to proceed should be taken without delay. Lack of agreement may not be used as justification for a more severe sentence in subsequent criminal justice proceedings.

16. Failure to implement an agreement made in the course of a restorative process should be referred back to the restorative programme or to the criminal justice authorities and a decision as to how to proceed should be taken without delay. Failure to implement the agreement may not be used as justification for a more severe sentence in subsequent criminal justice proceedings.

IV. Facilitators

17. Facilitators should be recruited from all sections of society and should generally possess good understanding of local cultures and communities. They should be able to demonstrate sound judgement and interpersonal skills necessary to conducting restorative processes.

18. Facilitators should perform their duties in an impartial manner, based on the facts of the case and on the needs and wishes of the parties. They should always respect the dignity of the parties and ensure that the parties act with respect towards each other.

19. Facilitators should be responsible for providing a safe and appropriate environment for the restorative process. They should be sensitive to any vulnerability of the parties.

20. Facilitators should receive initial training before taking up facilitation duties and should also receive in-service training. The training should aim at providing skills in conflict resolution,

Continued

taking into account the particular needs of victims and offenders, at providing basic knowledge of the criminal justice system and at providing a thorough knowledge of the operation of the restorative programme in which they will do their work.

V.   Continuing development of restorative justice programmes

21.   There should be regular consultation between criminal justice authorities and administrators of restorative justice programmes to develop a common understanding of restorative processes and outcomes, to increase the extent to which restorative programmes are used and to explore ways in which restorative approaches might be incorporated into criminal justice practices.

22.   Member States should promote research on and evaluation of restorative justice programmes to assess the extent to which they result in restorative outcomes, serve as an alternative to the criminal justice process and provide positive outcomes for all parties.

23.   Restorative justice processes may need to undergo change in concrete form over time. Member States should therefore encourage regular, rigorous evaluation and modification of such programmes in the light of the above definitions.

Source: United Nations Economic and Social Council. "Basic Principles on the Use of Restorative Justice Programmes in Criminal Matters." © 2000, United Nations. Reprinted with the permission of the United Nations.

SUGGESTIONS FOR FURTHER READING

Borrows, John. *Freedom and Indigenous Constitutionalism.* Toronto: University of Toronto Press, 2016.

Community Justice Initiatives (CJI). *The Elmira Case.* Roscoe Films, 2015. <https://cjiwr.com/the-elmira-case/>. Accessed March 29, 2019.

Internet Journal of Restorative Justice. <https://www.theogavrielides.com/ijrj>.

Justice Canada. "Brief Overview of Restorative Justice." <http://www.justice. gc.ca/eng/rp-pr/csj-sjc/jsp-sjp/rr00_16/p2.html>.

Kaufman, Amy. "Restorative Justice: New Ways to Look at Old Ideas." (2016) 41 *Can L Libr Rev* 12.

Shaw, M., and F. Jané. *Restorative Justice and Policing in Canada: Bringing the Community into Focus*. Ottawa: Royal Canadian Mounted Police, 1998.

Zehr, Howard. *The Little Book of Restorative Justice*. Intercourse, PA: Good Books, 2002.

ENDNOTES

1. The target group varies depending on the model and the legal system in which restorative justice is implemented. For example, the New Zealand Family Group Conferencing model is open to the youth justice coordinator, offender, offender's council and family, victim and victim's family and support system, whereas the Australian Wagga model is open to the Family Group Conferencing coordinator, offender and family, victim and family, and the investigating officer.

2. For instance, the Kapauku of New Zealand, the Nuer, the Middle Atlas tribes, the Egyptian Bedouin, and the Yonga tribe of Zambia (Walker and Davidson).

3. We focus on individual professional obligations, though the ethical infrastructure to adequately support restorative justice is probably best also thought of as including organizational features, as set out, for example, in Susan Sharpe, "Walking the Talk."

REFERENCES

Advocates' Society. *Guide for Lawyers Working with Indigenous Peoples*. 2018, May 8. <https://www.advocates.ca/Upload/Files/PDF/Advocacy/ BestPracticesPublications/Guide_for_Lawyers_Working_with_ Indigenous_Peoples_may16.pdf>. Accessed March 22, 2019.

Anand, Anita. "The Enforcement of Financial Market Crimes in Canada and the United Kingdom," in Carol Alexander and Douglas Cumming, editors, *Corruption and Fraud in Financial Markets: Malpractice, Misconduct and Manipulation*. Hoboken, NJ: Wiley Press, 2019.

Braithwaite, J. *Restorative Justice & Responsive Regulation*. Oxford: Oxford University Press, 2002 [Braithwaite, *Responsive Regulation*].

Braithwaite, J. "Restorative Justice and De-Professionalization." (2004) 13:1 *The Good Society* 28–31 [Braithwaite, "De-Professionalization"].

Brown, J. "The Use of Mediation to Resolve Criminal Cases: A Procedural Critique." (1994) 43 *Emory L J* 1247–1309.

Cawsey, R. A. "Task Force on the Criminal Justice System and Its Impact on the Indian and Metis People of Alberta." Edmonton: Government of Alberta, 1996.

Charbonneau, S. "6th International Conference on Restorative Justice." 6th International Conference on Restorative Justice. Leuven, Belgium: University of Leuven, 2003.

Community Justice Initiatives (CJI). *The Elmira Case*. Roscoe Films, 2015. <https://cjiwr.com/the-elmira-case/>. Accessed March 29, 2019.

Cormier, R. "Restorative Justice: Directions and Principles—Developments in Canada." 11th Session of the Commission on Crime Prevention and Criminal Justice. Vienna, Austria: International Centre for Criminal Law Reform and Criminal Justice Policy, 2002.

Criminal Code of Canada RSC 1985, c, C-46 [*Criminal Code*].

Department of Justice (Canada; DOJ). *Restorative Justice in Canada: A Consultation Paper*. Ottawa: Government of Canada, 2000.

Doak, J. and O'Mahony, D., "Evaluating the Success of Restorative Justice Conferencing," in T. Gavrielides, editor, *Routledge International Handbook of Restorative Justice*. New York, NY: Routledge. 2018.

Eglash, A. "Beyond Restitution: Creative Restitution," in J. Hudson and B. Galaway, editors, *Restitution in Criminal Justice*. Lexington, MA: DC Heath and Company, 1977.

Gavrielides, T. *Restorative Justice Theory & Practice: Addressing the Discrepancy*. Helsinki: HEUNI, 2007 [Gavrielides, *Theory & Practice*].

Gavrielides, T. "Restorative Justice: The Perplexing Concept. Conceptual Fault Lines and Power Battles within the Restorative Justice Movement." (2008) 8:2 *Criminol Crim Justice* 165–183 [Gavrielides, "Restorative Justice"].

Gavrielides, T. "Restorative Practices: From the Early Societies to the 1970s." (2011) *Internet Journal of Criminology* [Gavrielides, "Restorative Practices"].

Gavrielides, T. "The Victims' Directive and What Victims Want from Restorative Justice." (2015) *Victims and Offenders Journal.* doi:10.1080/15 564886.2014.982778 [Gavrielides, "The Victims' Directive"].

Gavrielides, T. *Routledge International Handbook of Restorative Justice.* London: Routledge, 2018 [Gavrielides, *Handbook*].

Gavrielides, T. "Victims and the Restorative Justice Ambition: A London Case Study of Potentials, Assumptions and Realities." (2018) *Contemp Justice Rev* [Gavrielides, "London Case Study"].

Government of Canada. *Youth Justice Strategy.* Ottawa: Government of Canada, 1998.

House of Commons. *Taking Responsibility: Report of the Standing Committee on Justice and Solicitor General on Its Review of Sentencing, Conditional Release and Related Aspects of Corrections.* Ottawa: Supply and Services Canada, 1988.

Kakekagamick, 2006 28549 ONCA CanLII.

Llewellyn, J., and R. Howse. *Restorative Justice: A Conceptual Framework.* Ottawa: Law Commission of Canada, 1998.

R v Gladue, [1999] 1 SCR 688 [*Gladue*].

R v Ipeelee, [2012] 1 SCR 433 [*Ipeelee*].

R v Kreko, 2016 ONCA 367 CanLII [*Kreko*].

R v Wells, 2000 SCC 10 CanLII [*Wells*].

Roberts, Julian V. "Sentencing, Public Opinion and the News Media." (1995) 26:1 *Revue Générale de droit* 115–125. doi:10.7202/1035852ar.

Sharpe, Susan. *Walking the Talk: Developing Ethics Frameworks for the Practice of Restorative Justice.* Langley, BC: Fraser Region Community Justice Initiatives Association, 2011. <http://cjibc.org/Walking_the_Talk_WEB.pdf>. Accessed March 31, 2019.

Simmonds, C. "Victims and Restorative Justice: Are Victims Re-victimised?" (2000) *The Caveat Report.*

Solicitor General Canada. *Corrections Population Growth: Report of the Federal/Provincial/Territorial Ministers Responsible for Justice.* Ottawa: Government of Canada, 1996.

Solicitor General Canada. *Corrections Population Growth: First Report on Progress for the Federal/Provincial/Territorial Ministers Responsible for Justice.* Ottawa: Government of Canada, 1997.

Solicitor General Canada. *Corrections Population Growth: Second Report on Progress for the Federal/Provincial/Territorial Ministers Responsible for Justice.* Ottawa: Government of Canada, 1998.

Solicitor General Canada. *Corrections Population Growth: Fourth Report on Progress for the Federal/Provincial/Territorial Ministers Responsible for Justice.* Ottawa: Government of Canada, 2000.

Twins v Canada. (Attorney General), (2016) 357 Federal Court CanLII.

United Nations Economic and Social Council. "Basic Principles on the Use of Restorative Justice Programmes in Criminal Matters." 2000. <https://www.un.org/ruleoflaw/blog/document/basic-principles-on-the-use-of-restorative-justice-programmes-in-criminal-matters/>. Accessed March 31, 2019.

Van Ness, D., and K. Strong. *Restoring Justice.* Cincinnati, OH: Anderson Publishing Company, 1997.

Victims' Bill of Rights, SC 2015, c 13.

Walker, L. & Davidson, J., "Restorative Justice Reentry Planning for the Imprisoned: An Evidence-Based Approach to Recidivism Reduction," in T. Gavrielides, editor, *The Routledge International Handbook of Restorative Justice.* New York, NY: Routledge. 2018.

Youth Criminal Justice Act, SC 2002, c 1 [YCJA].

Zehr, H. *Changing Lenses: A New Focus for Crime and Justice.* Scottdale, PA: Herald Press, 2005.

Zehr, H. *Changing Lenses: Restorative Justice for Our Times.* Kitchener, ON: Herald Press, 2015.

PART III

Conflict Resolution and Career Development

CHAPTER 6

Surviving and Thriving: Well-being, Competence, Difficult People, and Discrimination

You want to change your life? Change the way you think.
—Harvey Specter, *Suits*

LEARNING OBJECTIVES

After reading this chapter, students should understand:

- Mental health challenges in Canadian legal culture
- Professionalism, competence, ethics, and the need for self-care
- How balanced health and mindfulness can enhance effective conflict resolution
- Tips for maintaining well-being
- Strategies for dealing with difficult people in law
- Systemic discrimination challenges to legal professionals, based on things like race and gender

OVERVIEW

This concluding chapter focusses on the professional lives of criminal legal services professionals. We identify several broad issues in Canadian legal culture and suggest ways forward for individuals to maintain their physical and mental health; to better their workplaces; and to address interpersonal, work-life, and systemic conflicts that impact upon their lives and careers. The previous chapters have discussed how the personal well-being and mental state of those involved in criminal law negotiation and resolution are a vitally important part of effective conflict management and ethical practice. Our focus in this chapter is on research, but, as we will see, the issues we identify and discuss affect virtually everyone in Canadian criminal law, so many of our observations and conclusions apply broadly throughout the system.

Unfortunately, it has been widely recognized that lawyers are consistent "winners" of titles such as "professionals most likely to become depressed," in the sense that they are more likely than many other professions to burn out (Schiltz). Having said this, we believe that mindful self-care and an awareness of broader systemic issues can help professionals improve their own health and work environments. Many of our suggestions can also assist to improve reasoning, and the capacity for judgement by more constructively building resilience to manage stress (Cooper *et al.*). This chapter also discusses "sustainability" in professional practice, particularly through work-life management, self-care (Farrow),[1] and a better understanding of how some systemic issues can affect people at work. In particular, this last chapter explores practical challenges faced by lawyers. The current health crisis in Canadian law serves as a departure point for a discussion about the connection between good health and judgement, professionalism, and ethical obligations of all legal professionals.

We also further explore the issue of dealing with personal challenges from others. While we suggested in an earlier chapter that these issues might be a matter of both style and strategy, it's also true that for many reasons some people are just more difficult to deal with. This section explores issues relating to aggressive opposing counsel or others, then considers workplace stress in general. It provides a reality check, offering intersectional consideration of contextual factors such as race, gender, and other dimensions of embodied social location that affect the life experiences of legal services professionals differently. Finally, the chapter provides practical advice to lawyers and legal services professionals for avoiding burnout, and uses a literary case study, a look at a historical novella by Herman Melville, to illustrate aspects of job burnout and workplace stress, which have been observable in legal culture for some time.

In writing this chapter, we can confirm anecdotally based on our experiences and those observed amongst friends and colleagues that it is possible to live a healthy, happy, fulfilled, and meaningful life in the law. This chapter seeks to suggest a few ways to do this: ways that everyone working to resolve criminal law matters can more holistically live their "best lives" in the law, through an informed and mindful approach to work-life balance.

THE MENTAL HEALTH CRISIS IN LAW AND LEGAL CULTURE

Despite the stigma that has traditionally been attached to mental illness (Jolly-Ryan), its importance and pervasiveness is being increasingly acknowledged across contemporary society as part of the overall health and well-being needs of everyone. However, the study and practice of law, legal culture (Fish), and issues faced by those resolving criminal law matters can present distinct challenges. These challenges have negative implications involving the adverse effects of dealing with criminal law matters for a range of justice system participants, including students, advocates, and adjudicators, but others too, like jurors, police, and corrections workers.

For advocates, the institutions of legal culture, including law schools themselves, may be part of the problem (Seto). In fact, the process of "learning to think like a lawyer" can have significant psychological impacts; this has been compared to the kind of indoctrination that occurs in military boot camps (Dodek).[2] In fact, the dominant pedagogical techniques for learning law may themselves attract people with negative outlooks. In this respect, the process of "explaining law" often seems to privilege a very pessimistic outlook (Seligman *et al.*, 56).

When we were at law school, one of our classmates used to joke in learning torts, the study of civil wrongs, that "it's the class that proves your mother was right!" Their point was a general statement describing stereotypical parental nagging of children who engage in foolish risk and are regularly told things like "if you do that, you are going to lose an eye!" In youth, such warnings might have seemed a bit hyperbolic, and could pretty easily be dismissed as exaggerated concern. But in law, learning about how often things go unusually awry gives proof for the old saying that "truth is stranger than fiction." All lawyers require the capacity to foresee and estimate these risks, even if it seems at the end of a chain of a very unlikely series of occurrences. In this sense, the predominant study of law is consequently a bit pathological because it focusses on circumstances where things have gone wrong—and often very badly wrong, especially when considering the kinds of issues that arise in the criminal context, such as assault and murder and other serious offences.

The attraction of the subject to those who may be inclined towards negative thinking (Sheldon and Krieger), combined with the pessimistic explanatory style in teaching the subject may be part of the problem. This pedagogical approach still dominates law and could be some of what underlies the recognition in the last generation of significant mental health challenges among professionals in the legal system (Seto). But it's not just students or lawyers[3] who face increased mental health concerns in Canadian legal culture.

Involvement in criminal law proceedings may render participants at many levels particularly vulnerable to vicarious trauma, compassion fatigue, and post-traumatic stress (Moulton). Graphic details from the most gruesome crimes can adversely affect anyone, but those charged with responsibility to implement criminal law have little choice but to deal with the psychological effects of exposure to such evidence and testimony. The significance of these challenges in criminal law has been formally recognized at a number of levels.

For example, in 2017, the Ontario provincial government launched a program to provide counselling to jurors who face having to deal with the traumatic impacts of these proceedings (Hendry). In other recent developments, in 2018 the federal government passed legislation recognizing the need to address post-traumatic stress for, among others, corrections workers and RCMP officers (*Federal Framework on Post-Traumatic Stress Disorder Act*).[4] What's clear is that the potential for vicarious trauma can affect everyone involved: lawyers, mediators, other ADR professions, and courtroom personnel, including judges (Jaffe *et al.*). The stress from vicarious trauma and depression in dealing with legal proceedings has been acknowledged to have touched adjudicators at even the highest levels of Canada's courts, including a Chief Justice in Ontario (Moulton), and a former Supreme Court of Canada Judge (Brown, "He Didn't Have a Choice").

Increased efforts to recognize mental health as a serious issue in legal practice are grounded in a growing body of research that illustrates that self-care amongst criminal law professionals is in dire need of attention. On the one hand, it's clear there is emotional trauma associated with the exposure we face when dealing with the criminal cases before us. At the same time, we often work gruelling hours in an inherently adversarial environment (CBA, "Survey"), and the conditions of that workplace pose their own mental health challenges. It has long been known to psychologists that lawyers and legal services professionals in these circumstances are particularly vulnerable to stress and burnout (Kobasa).

For legal advocates, a further complicating factor is revealed by a 2017 study that found a "paradox" where higher-achieving lawyers, by monetary and status measures, had diminished mental health scores: the more successful a lawyer is in the eyes of the world, the more likely they are to suffer adverse psychological effects related to work (Koltai). This study raises the question of whether it is possible to both be a successful legal services professional working in criminal law and also be a happy, fulfilled person. We would argue that yes, this is achievable, but only if we redefine success to include what has been called the "third metric" (Huffington), measuring quality of life in the form of "human capital," as well as money and status, to judge professional success.

Conflict resolution is a set of human interactions. The capacity to function effectively to resolve conflicts can be impaired by mental health challenges that may also be correlated with things like fatigue, stress, and overwork. As we noted in Chapter 2, self-care is an important aspect of acting judiciously and fairly. In our experience, well-balanced conflict resolution professionals are less likely to act on their biases, and far less likely to escalate workplace conflicts with their colleagues, opposing counsel, and court staff. Effective life and career management practices are therefore not the "icing on the cake" for lawyers, to be sought once they have attained career success. In our view, balanced self-care is one key to "sustainable professionalism" (Farrow), and foundational to competent and effective conflict resolution in law. As an important part of professionalism, self-care also involves competence and other ethical issues, which we turn to in the next section.

LEGAL ETHICS: COMPETENCE AND SELF-CARE

All regulated legal professionals have a duty to be competent.[5] The broader ethical duty of competence also likely includes the capacity to demonstrate cultural skills and technical proficiency, as we discussed in Chapter 3. Important skills and behaviours that form part of the broader ethical obligation also includes other abilities, like civility in professional communications. For lawyers, the specific regulatory duty of competence means being someone who "has and applies relevant knowledge, skills and attributes in a manner appropriate to each matter undertaken on behalf of a client and the nature and terms of the lawyer's engagement" (FLSC, *Model Code,* r 3.1; see Appendix), and also includes a list of specific abilities, such as:

    i. legal research;
   ii. analysis;
  iii. application of the law to the relevant facts;
  iv. writing and drafting;
   v. negotiation;
  vi. alternative dispute resolution;
 vii. advocacy; and,
viii. problem solving.

The lawyer definition also contains descriptions and commentary on a range of professional obligations that involve a capacity for reflective self-assessment like "recognizing limitations in one's ability to handle a matter" and "managing one's practice effectively" (FLSC, *Model Code*, r 3.1).

All health issues can present significant challenges to professional competency. Poor health is especially problematic when it is exacerbated by the kinds of charged interpersonal interactions and stress that often occur in criminal proceedings, and can have adverse effects on professional reasoning and decision-making. It's worth noting that even today, many commonly assert what is now recognized to be a false dichotomy between mental and physical well-being. Most now acknowledge that all health issues occur on a spectrum that shows a close link between physiological and psychological conditions: "without mental health there can be no true physical health."[6] Consequently, wellness involves both the mind and the body.

This is actually wonderful news: self-care, fitness, health, and wellness do not magically result from being an excellent lawyer, mediator, paralegal, or other legal professional. Rather, self-care is essential and complementary to sustainable success in legal practice. In our view, more consistent professional performance, along with long-term career success in terms of satisfaction and happiness, is not possible without attention to our own well-being, and that of our professional colleagues.[7]

So, this is official permission, if you were looking for it. Go ahead. Practice taking superb care of yourself so that you can better serve your clients, and ultimately serve the interests of justice. Working in law, and helping to advance and defend people's most basic rights requires professional ability, but it does not demand a "counsel of perfection" (FLSC, *Model Code*, r 3.1-2, Commentary [15]; Harrison). Notice that the description of the work of advocates is usually called professional "practice." The fact is that excelling in any advocacy role takes time and effort. Similarly, wellness and self-care also requires patience, attention, consistent effort, and dedication. However, there are some simple things people can do to improve their well-being, which also implicitly recognize the interrelation between mental and physical health. These include:

- eating a well-balanced diet;
- staying hydrated;
- not skipping meals;

- maintaining a healthy weight;
- engaging in regular aerobic activity;
- getting sufficient sleep and rest to allow the body to recuperate including,
  - avoiding stimulants;
  - creating a comfortable sleep environment;
  - following a regular sleep schedule;
- maintaining social outlets;
- having a support structure in place, such as family and friends;
- having interests and/or hobbies outside of legal work field;
- incorporating daily mindfulness practices, including practising relaxation techniques such as meditation and deep diaphragmatic breathing;
- reducing or eliminating the use or abuse of alcohol, tobacco/nicotine, or caffeine; and
- monitoring the use of prescribed drugs to guard against either dependence or addiction (CBA, "Wellness").

We end this section on a note of caution in relation to the discussion of wellness and mental health above, and with respect to our suggestions for self-care throughout this chapter. Self-care and mindfulness are important strategies for maintaining balance. As we've noted, professionals working in criminal law may be at higher risk for developing a range of health challenges, including serious psychological illnesses like depression (Koltai). On this point, it's also important to acknowledge that not every situation is one that any legal services professional working in criminal law can address on their own.

Lawyers and legal services professionals should not hesitate to seek help from Employee Assistance Programs (EAPs), family doctors, and mental health crisis lines. Self-care strategies can be helpful in many circumstances. But in seeking to be healthier, or in contributing to the health of your workplace and that of your colleagues, there is no substitute for seeking the assistance of health care professionals, who may be in the best position to assess the nature, prognosis, and treatment of serious health concerns.

CHALLENGING CLIENT SITUATIONS AND AGGRESSIVE OPPOSING COUNSEL

Anyone who has been near a courtroom has probably witnessed the occasionally tense interactions among parties to proceedings and can appreciate that dealing with difficult people is a routine task faced by everyone in the criminal law. Criminal proceedings can often present dynamic and often unpredictable circumstances, involving individuals playing multiple roles. It may seem counterintuitive, but our experience suggests the accused is often among the least problematic individual in this setting.

For example, opposing counsel, witnesses, and allied professionals can also be difficult to work with. In Chapter 1, we discussed negotiation and highlighted several tactics for separating what appear as difficult or challenging individuals from the problem at hand. However, we largely left the very real question of what to do when the people themselves *are* the problem.

The following is a summary of suggestions for dealing with difficult people. These ideas are offered by negotiation theorist William Ury in his book *Getting Past No: Dealing with Difficult People*. Ury's central argument is that we can best diffuse high conflict interactions with difficult people by reframing the confrontation into a mutual attempt to solve a problem. Many of his suggestions are directly relevant to the wide range of advocates and other professionals working in criminal law.

1. First, control yourself—Ury recommends "going to the balcony" when faced with a difficult opponent. We need to be mindful about not letting others "push our buttons." Recognize what is emotionally triggering for you. Try not to react in the moment; to the extent that you can, distance yourself emotionally and view the situation objectively. Shift focus away from their conduct to the underlying interests of your client or your case and consider your best alternative to a negotiated agreement (BATNA). It may not be worth negotiating with someone who is being combative or difficult. Try to pause mindfully to consider the situation objectively.

2. Then, disarm the opponent by taking a "step to their side." Try to use and elicit the word "yes" to create an atmosphere of agreement, rather than contradiction. Try to reframe your role as one of active listener, trying to understand why they are taking a problematic position or tone. Ask clarifying questions and paraphrase their statements by reflecting them back. Acknowledge their points and feelings. Indicate empathy for their situation, and apologize if it is appropriate in the circumstances.

3. Try to refocus the conversation on interests, not positions. It may be helpful to ask open-ended questions that are oriented to solving problems. Try to introduce new options without directly challenging the other party's position. Look for solutions by using phrases like "what if," "why not," and "why." Questions introduce new options without directly challenging the opponent's position. Position-based negotiating tactics can be handled by ignoring questions, or by reformulating them. It may also be helpful to explicitly identify the problematic behaviour by stating that it was difficult or troubling.

4. "Build them a golden bridge" by giving them choices, suggesting and helping craft solutions that they are able to buy into. To the extent that it is possible, ask them for their ideas and constructive criticism. An opponent's resistance may indicate that they still has unmet interests. Try to give them space and time to reframe the proposed solution as beneficial to them.

5. Offer them the opportunity to say no. Ury writes: "Instead of using power to bring your opponent to his knees, use it to bring him to his senses" (113). Invite them into understanding what will happen if an agreement is not reached, without confronting them. Ask them reality-testing questions.

GENDER, EQUALITY, AND DISCRIMINATION

One further issue related to conflict resolution in criminal law relates to the well-being of individual professionals based on their personal characteristics and the individual effects of systemic challenges.

In Chapter 3, we discussed a cognitive error called the fundamental attributional error. That is the mistake in thinking, in relation to accused defendants, that explains potentially criminal behaviour largely as the result of internal factors, like flawed or bad character. This bias in thinking about human behaviour, which can apply to anyone, can also have effects on those who work in criminal law. In this respect we have to be mindful that some things are beyond personal control, for ourselves and others, and are the result of external circumstances.

Mindfulness and self-care are very amenable to individual action. But just as there are some physical and mental health issues that require professional intervention, there are also systemic issues that can affect legal services professionals who resolve criminal disputes. We've previously talked about how the adversarial nature of criminal law proceedings, dealing with challenging clients, or just difficult people can contribute to stressful dysfunction in the work environment. As a broader issue, those who work in law also face the potential for systemic discrimination, based on personal characteristics like gender and race. Discrimination against legal professionals on these grounds has a long history in Canada.

For example, women have faced particular challenges in Canadian legal culture. Up until almost the 20th century, women were prevented from obtaining legal training. The first woman to practise law in Canada was Clara Brett Martin, who had to petition the Ontario Legislature for the passage of special statutes to be called to the Bar (Backhouse, *Petticoats and Prejudice*, 293–326, 334). It has only been in the last generation that enrolments of women have outnumbered those of men in Canadian law schools.

Despite this apparent progress towards gender diversity, researchers have documented the fact that women in the legal profession often face harassment and discrimination (Backhouse, "Gender and Race," 213–221). Today, female lawyers face many challenges, including lower pay, more family care responsibilities, and increased workplace and sexual harassment. One effect of these challenges is the disproportionate rate of attrition for women who leave law (Kay *et al.*, "Turning Points and Transitions"), and modern commentators continue to note the lingering effects of what appear to be deeply embedded and persistent discriminatory practices (Kay *et al.*, "Undermining Gender Equality").

Similar discrimination and equality issues based on race and religion have traditionally been experienced by others in the Canadian legal community. Today, Robert Sutherland is acknowledged to have been the first Black lawyer to be called to the Bar in Canada in 1855. Sutherland was a graduate of Queen's College in Kingston, Ontario, and later practised law in Walkerton, Ontario. Despite Sutherland's pioneering achievement (Brown, "Robert Sutherland"), later Black law students were few and far between (Backhouse, "Gender and Race," 2–7). Jewish law students also faced widespread discrimination, battling anti-Semitism and active opposition to their entry into the legal profession. One commentator notes, for example, that, as students-at-law through the early 20th century, Black students "typically worked only for other Blacks, or Jewish lawyers—neither Blacks nor Jews, it seems, fit the 'professional' mould" (Backhouse, "Gender and Race," 2–7). Similar barriers to accessing legal education were also faced by other groups throughout Canada, such as Aboriginals and Asians (Brockman, 519–525).

One recent report from the legal regulator in Ontario suggests that discriminatory attitudes and practices of the past continue to have adverse effects (LSO). Looking at racialized lawyers and paralegal licensees, it found that

> racialization establishes a measurable constellation of career challenges for racialized licensees that are distinct from those of their not-racialized colleagues: challenges that are rooted in their racialized status as well as many related challenges that are compounded and amplified. (LSO, 77)

Everyone faces challenges in both life and the workplace. It is important to acknowledge and address the reality that people inevitably experience work-life conflicts. But because of systemic issues, some may face more issues. Many people also have only limited access to opportunities for self-care, depending on their situation. Based on things like health status, socio-economic conditions, education, and social opportunities, which are themselves often rooted in things like race and gender, some have more and better resources, as well as readier access to effective support mechanisms. While we can, and should, individually push against traditional boundaries with reference to things like gender roles, racial and other biases, and stereotyping, these systemic challenges with social inequity have certainly not been surmounted in either the legal profession,[8] or arguably within Canada's broader legal culture.

CASE STUDY: *Bartleby the Scrivener*

Consider a case study of lawyer and legal service provider, self-care, and mental health, from an iconic work of historical fiction: Herman Melville's 1853 story *Bartleby the Scrivener: A Story of Wall Street.* In Melville's story, the character of Bartleby can be read as a historical literary recognition of the destructive effects of a lack of self-care on professional life, in law and affiliated professions. Ultimately, it becomes a story about depression, isolation, and loneliness.

The title character, Bartleby, works on Wall Street as a law copyist, a historical form of law clerk called a "scrivener," a traditional role that was often filled by an apprentice or associate to a lawyer. The story is narrated by a lawyer who supervises Bartleby. Initially, Bartleby works hard as a scrivener, producing handwritten copies of the lawyer's documents at their office on Wall Street. However, Bartleby's health and work product deteriorate over time.

Bartleby's conduct devolves into increasingly anti-social behaviour, which is accepted for a long time because of his high level of productivity and its benefits to the firm. He begins to starve himself; he stops speaking to others; he starts to sleep at his desk. Bartleby loses all interest in activities outside of work. His apathy becomes his catchphrase, as he repeats woefully, "I'd prefer not to." Ultimately, Bartleby has a complete breakdown and is institutionalized. At the end of the story, the narrator relates that Bartleby had previously worked in a "dead letter" office, a place where undeliverable mail is destroyed.

Case Study Discussion

There are several ways that literary theorists have read Bartleby, but one plausible reading that speaks to our contemporary time, in the context

Continued

of legal services professionals working in the legal profession, is that the author uses the character of Bartleby to warn against the dangers of endless toil at sedentary legal work, in which the worker finds remuneration but no meaning. Indeed, the character's breakdown, described in fiction long before contemporary mental health research provided insight into the details of depressive disorders, fits neatly into the criteria for a major depressive episode.

A question for reflection in pondering one's career, not to be answered right now necessarily, but to be considered over the coming years might be as follows: How do we avoid Bartleby's fate? How can we be sure not to end up like him, starved for all but work, alone, unloved, and disinterested in our lives?

SUMMARY AND CONCLUSION

In sum, this chapter has looked at how prioritizing self-care, and acknowledging and addressing health challenges can ensure that lawyers and legal services professionals optimize their effectiveness at conflict resolution while living their best lives. More specifically, it has discussed ways in which self-care is important for effective conflict resolution. It connected self-care by legal professionals to professional ethical obligations, considered issues posed by workplace stress, and conveyed concerns with lawyer mental health and how to get help.

The chapter has also outlined strategies for dealing with difficult clients and unreasonable opposing counsel. We also critically explored ways in which social location is relevant to professional practice. We extended our exploration of systemic challenges in Canadian law to consider those presented by broader issues of discrimination and its effects on individual professionals based on things like gender and race. Last, we presented a literary look at the work-life challenges, to encourage reflection on the personal risks and potential benefits of careers in law.

To conclude, there may be nothing more apt to do than reference Plato's *Republic*. Written in Greece in 380 BCE, it is one of the most influential classical texts on political and legal philosophy. It explores what constitutes a just polity and what conduct is ethical if undertaken by citizens. The book ends with the Myth of Er. This is Plato's fable about reincarnation, not intended to be taken literally but figuratively. In the myth, Odysseus, the greatest of the Ancient Greek heroes, is tasked with choosing a new life for his next incarnation. To quote the text,

> the soul of Odysseus drew the last lot of all and came to make its choice, and, from memory of its former toils having flung away ambition, went about for a long time in quest of the life of an ordinary citizen who minded his own business, and with difficulty found it lying in some corner disregarded by the others, and upon seeing it said that it would have done the same had it drawn the first lot, and chose it gladly.

Perhaps Plato answered the question of whether the choice to spend one's life working in the legal profession, in the criminal law context, could be a good life.

The choice made by Odysseus in Myth of Er echoes and foreshadows what research says about wellness for those working in the criminal justice system: doing work that allows for leisure and rest, that is not motivated either by a quest for fame or for fortune, but rather for the sake of meaningfully doing one's duty well. Solving problems and resolving conflicts as expeditiously and harmoniously as possible, according to contemporary scholarship about human happiness and wellness, can be as clear a path to a good life in the 21st-century context of work in the field of criminal law, just as it was in 380 BCE.

SUGGESTIONS FOR FURTHER READING

Bromwich, Rebecca. "Law Students: To Thrive in a Criminal Legal Career, Think 'Perennial'." *Robson Crim Legal Blog*, 2017, July 19. <https://www.robsoncrim.com/single-post/2017/07/19/Law-Students-To-Thrive-in-a-Criminal-Legal-Career-Think-%E2%80%9CPerennial%E2%80%9D>. Accessed April 5, 2019.

Melville, Herman. *Bartleby the Scrivener*. New York: Putnam, 1853.

Moulton, Donalee. "Understanding Burnout and Fixing It." (2011, April) *The Bottom Line.*

Organ, Jerome M. "What Do We Know about the Satisfaction/ Dissatisfaction of Lawyers? A Meta-Analysis of Research on Lawyer Satisfaction and Well-Being." (2011) 8 *U St Thomas L J* 225.

Plato. *Plato in Twelve Volumes,* translated by Paul Shorey. Cambridge, MA: Harvard University Press, 1969.

Telfer, Thomas G. W. "The Wellness Doctrines for Law Students & Young Lawyers, by Jerome Doraismy." (2017) 54:2 *Osgoode Hall L J* 645.

ENDNOTES

1. We consider only a small part of the larger concept of "sustainability" as a potentially innovative and constructive approach to law, as set out by Farrow.

2. "Legal education is very much a socialization process. To a degree, it shares certain commonalities with the army. Both attempt to inculcate the young and to strip the would-be soldier/lawyer of his/her previous affiliations. Neither legal education nor the military values true diversity," Dodek, at 122.

3. One massive 2016 study of over 12,000 American lawyers found rates of depression more than three times higher than the general population, and a statistically heightened occurrence of anxiety; see Krill *et al.* For comparisons to the Canadian context, see Seto; Fish.

4. The *Federal Framework* also recognizes military personnel, first responders, and firefighters.

5. In addition to lawyer rules set out in professional codes (see FLSC, *Model Code*), this group of regulated legal professionals in Canada also includes Ontario paralegals and British Columbia notaries; see rule 4, Society of Notaries Public of British Columbia, as well as Notaires in the province of Quebec.

6. Dr. Brock Chisholm of the World Health Organization was among the first to advance this idea; see WHO.

7. The lawyer professional rules highlight the obligation of other lawyers to encourage counsel who face physical, mental, emotional conditions, disorders, or addiction to seek assistance, and the duty to report any

misconduct arising from these circumstances; see FLSC, *Model Code*, r 7.1-3, Commentary [3].

8.   See, for example, the recent LSO report on the experiences of racialized lawyer licencees in Ontario.

REFERENCES

Backhouse, Constance. *Petticoats and Prejudice: Women and Law in Nineteenth Century Canada.* Toronto: Women's Press, 1991.

Backhouse, N. "Gender and Race in the Construction of 'Legal Professionalism': Historical Perspectives." Chief Justice of Ontario's Advisory Committee on Professionalism, 1st Colloquium, October 2004. <http://www.lsuc.on.ca/media/constance_backhouse_gender_ and_race.pdf> [Backhouse, "Gender and Race"].

Brockman, Joan. "Exclusionary Tactics: The History of Women and Visible Minorities in the Legal Profession in British Columbia," in Hamar Foster and John McLaren, editors, *Essays in the History of Canadian Law: British Columbia and the Yukon*, vol. 6. Toronto: The Osgoode Society, 1995, at 508.

Brown, Bonnie. "He Didn't Have a Choice: How Depression Cost Gerald Le Dain His Supreme Court Post." *CBC: Sunday Edition*, 2018, August 26. <https://www.cbc.ca/radio/thesundayedition/the-sunday-edition-january-14-2018-1.4471379/he-didn-t-have-a-choice-how-depression-cost-gerald-le-dain-his-supreme-court-post-1.4471385>. Accessed April 5, 2019 [Brown, "He Didn't Have a Choice"].

Brown, Deirdre Rowe. "Robert Sutherland: Celebrating the Legacy." (2009) 35:1 *Queen's L J* 401 [Brown, "Robert Sutherland"].

Canadian Bar Association (CBA). *Survey of Lawyers on Wellness Issues.* Report and Survey by Ipsos Reid for the Legal Profession Assistance Conference, 2012. <http://www.cba.org/CBAMediaLibrary/cba_na/ PDFs/CBA%20Wellness%20PDFs/FINAL-Report-on-Survey-of-Lawyers-on-Wellness-Issues.pdf>. Accessed April 5, 2019 [CBA, "Survey"].

Canadian Bar Association (CBA). "Wellness: Mental Health and Wellness in the Legal Profession." 2017. <MDcme.ca> [CBA, "Wellness"].

Cooper, C. L., P. J. Dewe, and M. P. O'Driscoll. *Organizational Stress: A Review and Critique of Theory, Research, and Applications*. Thousand Oaks, CA: Sage, 2001.

Dodek, Adam M. "Canadian Legal Ethics: A Subject in Search of Scholarship." (2000) 50 *UTLJ* 115.

Farrow, Trevor. "Sustainable Professionalism." (2008) 46:1 *Osgoode Hall L J* 51.

Federal Framework on Post-Traumatic Stress Disorder Act, SC 2018, c 13.

Federation of Law Societies. *Model Code of Professional Conduct* [FLSC, *Model Code*], as amended March 14, 2017. <https://flsc.ca/wp-content/uploads/2018/03/Model-Code-as-amended-March-2017-Final.pdf>. Accessed January 20, 2019.

Fish, Daniel. "The Mental-Health Crisis in Law." *Precedent Magazine*, 2018, March 6. <https://lawandstyle.ca/law/cover-story-the-mental-health-crisis-in-law/>. Accessed April 4, 2019.

Harrison, Thomas. "The Good, the Perfect, and the Professional: Reflections on the Tension between Principle and Practicality in Teaching Legal Ethics." 2017. <https://papers.ssrn.com/sol3/papers.cfm?abstract_id=2940259>.

Hendry, Mallory. "Ontario Announces Free Counselling Program for Jurors." *Canadian Lawyer Magazine*, 2017, February 1. <https://www.canadianlawyermag.com/legalfeeds/author/mallory-hendry/ontario-ag-announces-free-counselling-program-for-jurors-7279/>. Accessed April 5, 2019.

Huffington, Ariana. *Thrive: The Third Metric to Redefining Success and Creating a Life of Well-Being, Wisdom, and Wonder*. New York: Harmony Books, 2014.

Jaffe, Peter G., Claire V. Crooks, Billie Lee Dunford-Jackson, and Judge Michael Town. "Vicarious Trauma in Judges: The Personal Challenge of Dispensing Justice." (2009) 54 *Juvenile and Family Court Journal* 4.

Jolly-Ryan, Jennifer. "The Last Taboo: Breaking Law Students with Mental Illnesses and Disabilities Out of the Stigma Straitjacket." (2004) 79 *UMKC L Rev* 123.

Kay, Fiona M., Stacey Alarie, and Jones Adjei. "Undermining Gender Equality: Female Attrition from Private Law Practice." (2016) 50:3 *Law & Soc'y Rev* 766–801.

Kay, Fiona, et al., for the Law Society of Upper Canada. "Turning Points and Transitions: Women's Career's in the Legal Profession." 2004, September.

Kobasa, S. C. "Commitment and Coping in Stress Resistance among Lawyers." (1982) 42:4 *J Pers Soc Psychol* 707–717.

Koltai, Jonathan. "The Status-Health Paradox." (2018) 59:1 *J Health Soc Behav* 20–37.

Krill, Patrick R., Ryan Johnson, and Linda Albert. "The Prevalence of Substance Use and Other Mental Health Concerns among American Attorneys." (2016) 10:2 *J Addict Med* 46.

Law Society of Ontario (LSO). *Challenges Facing Racialized Licensees: Final Report*. 2014. <http://www.stratcom.ca/wp-content/uploads/manual/Racialized-Licensees_Full-Report.pdf>. Accessed April 11, 2019.

Moulton, Donalee. "Vicarious Trauma: The Cumulative Effects of Caring." *Canadian Lawyer Magazine*, 2015, February 2. <https://www.canadianlawyermag.com/article/vicarious-trauma-the-cumulative-effects-of-caring-2767/>. Accessed April 5, 2019.

Schiltz, Patrick J. "On Being a Happy, Healthy, and Ethical Member of an Unhappy, Unhealthy, and Unethical Profession." (1999) 52 *Vand L Rev* 880.

Seligman, Martin E. P., Paul R. Verkuil, and Terry H. Kang. "Why Lawyers Are Unhappy." (2001) 23 *Cardozo L Rev* 52.

Seto, Megan. "Killing Ourselves: Depression as an Institutional, Workplace and Professional Problem." (2012) 2:2 *Western Journ L Studies* 1.

Sheldon, Kennon M., and Lawrence S. Krieger. "Does Legal Education Have Undermining Effects on Law Students? Evaluating Changes in Motivation, Values and Well-Being." (2004) 22 *Behave Sci & L* 262.

Society of Notaries Public of British Columbia. *Principles of Ethical and Professional Conduct Guideline*. 2011. <https://www.notaries.bc.ca/resources/Upload/28-04-2011-13-36-13_Ethical%20and%20Professional%20Conduct_April2011.pdf>. Accessed April 7, 2019.

Ury, William. *Getting Past No: Dealing with Difficult People*. New York: Bantam, 1993.

World Health Organization. Outline for a Study Group on World Health and the Survival of the Human Race: Material Drawn from Articles and Speeches Made by Brock Chisholm C.B.E., M.D., Director General of the World Health Organization. 1954.

APPENDIX

FLSC *Model Code*, Excerpt on Lawyer Competence

3.1 COMPETENCE

Definitions

3.1-1 In this section,

   "Competent lawyer" means a lawyer who has and applies relevant knowledge, skills and attributes in a manner appropriate to each matter undertaken on behalf of a client and the nature and terms of the lawyer's engagement, including:

(a) knowing general legal principles and procedures and the substantive law and procedure for the areas of law in which the lawyer practises;

(b) investigating facts, identifying issues, ascertaining client objectives, considering possible options and developing and advising the client on appropriate courses of action;

(c) implementing as each matter requires, the chosen course of action through the application of appropriate skills, including:
   (i) legal research;
   (ii) analysis;
   (iii) application of the law to the relevant facts;
   (iv) writing and drafting;
   (v) negotiation;
   (vi) alternative dispute resolution;
   (vii) advocacy; and
   (viii) problem solving;

(d) communicating at all relevant stages of a matter in a timely and effective manner;

(e) performing all functions conscientiously, diligently and in a timely and cost-effective manner;

(f) applying intellectual capacity, judgment and deliberation to all functions;

(g) complying in letter and spirit with all rules pertaining to the appropriate professional conduct of lawyers;

(h) recognizing limitations in one's ability to handle a matter or some aspect of it and taking steps accordingly to ensure the client is appropriately served;

(i) managing one's practice effectively;

(j) pursuing appropriate professional development to maintain and enhance legal knowledge and skills; and

(k) otherwise adapting to changing professional requirements, standards, techniques and practices.

COMPETENCE

3.1-2 A lawyer must perform all legal services undertaken on a client's behalf to the standard of a competent lawyer.

Commentary

[1] As a member of the legal profession, a lawyer is held out as knowledgeable, skilled and capable in the practice of law. Accordingly, the client is entitled to assume that the lawyer has the ability and capacity to deal adequately with all legal matters to be undertaken on the client's behalf.

[2] Competence is founded upon both ethical and legal principles. This rule addresses the ethical principles. Competence involves more than an understanding of legal principles: it involves an adequate knowledge of the practice and procedures by which such principles can be effectively applied. To accomplish this, the lawyer should keep abreast of developments in all areas of law in which the lawyer practises.

[3]   In deciding whether the lawyer has employed the requisite degree of knowledge and skill in a particular matter, relevant factors will include:

(a)   the complexity and specialized nature of the matter;

(b)   the lawyer's general experience;

(c)   the lawyer's training and experience in the field;

(d)   the preparation and study the lawyer is able to give the matter; and

(e)   whether it is appropriate or feasible to refer the matter to, or associate or consult with, a lawyer of established competence in the field in question.

[4]   In some circumstances, expertise in a particular field of law may be required; often the necessary degree of proficiency will be that of the general practitioner.

[5]   A lawyer should not undertake a matter without honestly feeling competent to handle it, or being able to become competent without undue delay, risk or expense to the client. The lawyer who proceeds on any other basis is not being honest with the client. This is an ethical consideration and is distinct from the standard of care that a tribunal would invoke for purposes of determining negligence.

[6]   A lawyer must recognize a task for which the lawyer lacks competence and the disservice that would be done to the client by undertaking that task. If consulted about such a task, the lawyer should:

(a)   decline to act;

(b)   obtain the client's instructions to retain, consult or collaborate with a lawyer who is competent for that task; or

(c)   obtain the client's consent for the lawyer to become competent without undue delay, risk or expense to the client.

[7]   A lawyer should also recognize that competence for a particular task may require seeking advice from or collaborating with experts in scientific, accounting or other non-legal fields, and, when it is appropriate, the lawyer should not hesitate to seek the client's instructions to consult experts.

[7A]   When a lawyer considers whether to provide legal services under a limited scope retainer the lawyer must carefully assess in each case whether, under the circumstances, it is possible to render those services in a competent manner. An agreement for such services does not exempt a lawyer from the duty to provide competent representation. The lawyer should consider the legal knowledge, skill, thoroughness and preparation reasonably necessary for the representation. The lawyer should ensure that the client is fully informed of the nature of the arrangement and clearly understands the scope and limitation of the services. See also rule 3.2-1A.

[7B]   In providing short-term summary legal services under Rules 3.4-2A–3.4-2D, a lawyer should disclose to the client the limited nature of the services provided and determine whether any additional legal services beyond the short-term summary legal services may be required or are advisable, and encourage the client to seek such further assistance.

[8]   A lawyer should clearly specify the facts, circumstances and assumptions on which an opinion is based, particularly when the circumstances do not justify an exhaustive investigation and the resultant expense to the client. However, unless the client instructs otherwise, the lawyer should investigate the matter in sufficient detail to be able to express an opinion rather than mere comments with many qualifications. A lawyer should only express his or her legal opinion when it is genuinely held and is provided to the standard of a competent lawyer.

[9]   A lawyer should be wary of providing unreasonable or over-confident assurances to the client, especially when the lawyer's employment or retainer may depend upon advising in a particular way.

[10]   In addition to opinions on legal questions, a lawyer may be asked for or may be expected to give advice on non-legal matters such as the business, economic, policy or social complications involved in the question or the course the client should choose. In many instances the lawyer's experience will be such that the

lawyer's views on non-legal matters will be of real benefit to the client. The lawyer who expresses views on such matters should, if necessary and to the extent necessary, point out any lack of experience or other qualification in the particular field and should clearly distinguish legal advice from other advice.

[11] In a multi-discipline practice, a lawyer must ensure that the client is made aware that the legal advice from the lawyer may be supplemented by advice or services from a non-lawyer. Advice or services from non-lawyer members of the firm unrelated to the retainer for legal services must be provided independently of and outside the scope of the legal services retainer and from a location separate from the premises of the multi-discipline practice. The provision of non-legal advice or services unrelated to the legal services retainer will also be subject to the constraints outlined in the rules/by-laws/regulations governing multi-discipline practices.

[12] The requirement of conscientious, diligent and efficient service means that a lawyer should make every effort to provide timely service to the client. If the lawyer can reasonably foresee undue delay in providing advice or services, the client should be so informed.

[13] The lawyer should refrain from conduct that may interfere with or compromise his or her capacity or motivation to provide competent legal services to the client and be aware of any factor or circumstance that may have that effect.

[14] A lawyer who is incompetent does the client a disservice, brings discredit to the profession and may bring the administration of justice into disrepute.
      In addition to damaging the lawyer's own reputation and practice, incompetence may also injure the lawyer's partners and associates.

[15] Incompetence, Negligence and Mistakes—This rule does not require a standard of perfection. An error or omission, even though it might be actionable for damages in negligence or contract, will not necessarily constitute a failure to maintain

the standard of professional competence described by the rule. However, evidence of gross neglect in a particular matter or a pattern of neglect or mistakes in different matters may be evidence of such a failure, regardless of tort liability. While damages may be awarded for negligence, incompetence can give rise to the additional sanction of disciplinary action.

Source: Federation of Law Societies of Canada. *Model Code of Professional Conduct.* 2017. Reprinted with permission.

AUTHOR BIOGRAPHIES

Rebecca Jaremko Bromwich is a lawyer and legal academic whose practice, teaching, and research interests focus on criminal law and conflict resolution. She is Program Director for the Graduate Diploma in Conflict Resolution at Carleton University in Ottawa, Canada. Dr. Bromwich is also a *per diem* Crown Attorney. She has certificates in mediation and negotiation from Harvard Law School's Program on Negotiation. Rebecca received her Ph.D. in 2015 from the Carleton University Department of Law and Legal Studies, and was the first-ever graduate of that program. She also has an LL.M. and LL.B., received from Queen's University in 2002 and 2001 respectively, and holds a Graduate Certificate in Women's Studies from the University of Cincinnati. Rebecca is a co-editor of Robson Hall Law School's criminal law and justice blog (robsoncrim.com) and is a research associate with the UK's Restorative Justice for All Institute.

Thomas Harrison is a teacher and lawyer. He has taught legal ethics at Queen's University; animal law, critical thinking, and ethics at Durham College; and psychology at Seneca College, all in Ontario. Prior to studying law (Queen's, LL.B., 2001), Thomas was a social worker and taught at-risk youth in Toronto, after earning his B.Ed. from Queen's University (1992). Thomas articled with Mr. Justice Archie Campbell of Ontario's Superior Court (2001–2002), and later practised law with the Ministry of the Attorney General and Ontario's Office of the Chief Justice. From 2011 to 2012, he helped establish the provincial Death Investigation Oversight Committee, an independent body reviewing Coroner's complaints. He has worked as policy counsel with the Canadian Federation of Law Societies (2012–2013), and served as a lawyer member of Ontario's Consent and Capacity Board (2013–2015). He also has a Certificate in Adjudication from the Society of Adjudicators and Regulators (2012), and a Master's degree in Public Policy and Administration (Ryerson, 2007). Thomas is the author or editor of several articles and publications, and completed his Ph.D. dissertation at Queen's University in 2016, examining the role of independent lawyers and judges in Canada's justice system.

Theo Gavrielides is the Founder and Director of Restorative Justice for All (RJ4All), an international NGO working to advance community cohesion using the values and practices of restorative justice. He has also founded and directs the IARS International Institute. He is Adjunct Professor at the School of Criminology of Simon Fraser University (Canada), and Visiting Professor at Buckinghamshire New University (UK). Professor Gavrielides is Editor-in-Chief of the *International Journal of Human Rights in Healthcare*, *Youth Voice Journal*, and the *Internet Journal of Restorative Justice*. He is an advisor to the European Commission's security programs, and the coordinator of a number of EU-funded research projects on violent radicalization, migration, restorative justice, youth, and human rights. His publications include *Restorative Justice Theory and Practice* (2007), *Rights and Restoration within Youth Justice* (editor, 2012), *Reconstructing Restorative Justice Philosophy* (co-editor, 2013), and *The Philosophy of Restorative Justice* (editor, 2015). He also edited *Offenders No More* (2015) and *Restorative Justice, The Library of Essays on Justice* (2015), as well as *The Routledge International Handbook of Restorative Justice* (2018).